let your kids go wild outside

let your kids go wild outside

CREATIVE WAYS TO HELP CHILDREN DISCOVER NATURE AND ENJOY THE GREAT OUTDOORS

Fiona Bird

CICO BOOKS
LONDON NEW YORK

DEDICATION

This book is for my Mother, Joy Murray, a true animal lover, and my Mother-in-law, Rosemary Bird, who taught her grandchildren about birds. It is dedicated to the memory of my friend William McCosh, who knew so much about trees; my Father-in-law, Dickie Bird, who so enjoyed his bees; and my Father, John Murray, who wished he had known more about butterflies.

Published in 2016 by CICO Books
An imprint of Ryland Peters & Small Ltd

20–21 Jockey's Fields
London WC1R 4BW

341 E 116th St
New York, NY 10029

www.rylandpeters.com

10 9 8 7 6 5 4 3 2 1

Text © Fiona Bird 2016
Design and original photography © CICO Books 2016
All photography by Dylan Drummond, except for those images listed in the picture credits on page 160.

A CIP catalog record for this book is available from the Library of Congress and the British Library.

ISBN: 978 1 78249 313 6

Printed in China

Editor: Caroline West
Designer: Mark Latter
Photographers: Dylan Drummond and Terry Benson
Illustrator: Ian Youngs

In-house editor: Dawn Bates
In-house designer: Fahema Khanam
Art director: Sally Powell
Head of production: Patricia Harrington
Publishing manager: Penny Craig
Publisher: Cindy Richards

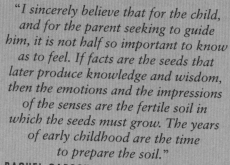

"I sincerely believe that for the child, and for the parent seeking to guide him, it is not half so important to know as to feel. If facts are the seeds that later produce knowledge and wisdom, then the emotions and the impressions of the senses are the fertile soil in which the seeds must grow. The years of early childhood are the time to prepare the soil."
RACHEL CARSON, MARINE BIOLOGIST AND CONSERVATIONIST (1907–1964)

A word of caution

Neither the author nor the publisher can accept any legal responsibitliy or liability for any harm arising from participating in the activities described in this book. The author and publisher also cannot be held responsible for, or be liable for, the erroneous consumption of wild plants (including mushrooms, fungi, and marine algae) that have caused severe or allergic reactions resulting from misidentification. The photographs and text in this book should not be used alone for identification purposes.

Contents

INTRODUCTION
Thoughts for Carers

The sight of bird's foot trefoil (*Lotus corniculatus*) on a cliff reminds me of a seaside picnic with my paternal grandmother when she called the flower by its common name "eggs and bacon." I still associate the flower's yellow and streaked red appearance with thoughts of breakfast but, more importantly, I learnt its common name. In *The Sense of Wonder*, Rachel Carson writes of a synergistic adult-child relationship that comes from shared time outdoors. *"If a child is to keep alive his inborn sense… he needs the companionship of at least one adult who can share it, rediscovering with him the joy, excitement and mystery of the world we live in."*

A CHANGING WORLD

For many, including the poet Seamus Heaney, picking blackberries releases a waterfall of late-summer childhood memories. Heaney's poem *Blackberry Picking* describes a simple countryside tradition as a major childhood event. Looking back is often coupled with the blurred vision of rose-tinted spectacles but, as a child, I recall cornflowers at the edges of fields. Today, most children won't find wild cornflowers. The cowslips (*Primula veris*) I picked for my grandparents on chalky downlands are now rare and certainly mustn't be gathered for a posy. Cowslips are on a Red Data List of endangered species.

Wild flowers aren't the only wild dilemma. Pollinators are also disappearing and global warming is threatening our marine and terrestrial ecosystems (see page 18). The words native, non-native, and invasive weren't in my childhood vocabulary; neither was the water-polluting nurdle (a small plastic pellet that marine life mistakenly feeds on). I have, however, no desire to bury my head in the sand in the hope that the pendulum will swing back to a world where there are no invasive species. Some may say it has always been thus—indeed, centuries ago many non-native North American plants and animals were introduced by European settlers. We, as carers, however, need to think about the relationship that we and our children have with today's natural world. In the United Kingdom, the ash tree (*Fraxinus* spp.) is suffering from ash dieback caused by the pathogen *Hymenoscyphus fraxineus* (see page 18). Meanwhile, the sycamore has naturalized in the UK and yet is considered an invasive species by some.

TEACHING KIDS TO LOVE NATURE

To a child the natural world is full of wonder and excitement. Adults must, of course, be mindful of complex environmental issues but at the same time maintain a child-like inquisitiveness. Through outdoor play and exploring the wild comes a desire for knowledge that gives real meaning to the facts of natural science. It is not a crime for an adult to be unable to name a flower or bird, but a shared learning opportunity for young and old. There are lessons to learn from local conservation rather than a broad-brush approach. I'm a devotee of Gilbert White, the 18th-century clergyman who recorded flora and fauna local to him (see page 11). This is a man who contributed hugely to our understanding of natural science without traveling many miles and certainly without air miles. Yes, modern science is helpful, but White used simple naturalist skills to identify the harvest mouse that scampers up an ear of wheat in the late-summer breeze. His skills were only unique in that he concentrated on living rather than dead species, which was the fashion. There isn't an app to replace a carer's lap and reading is certainly one way to instil a love of nature in children at an early age. If you look closely, you'll see that the illustrated tales of Beatrix Potter (see page 9) include mosses and fungi as well as wildlife. An adult can read the tale as a child looks at the illustrations. I've also included a "wild" book list for older children (see *Resources*, on page 157).

GETTING KIDS OUTDOORS

As a mother of six, I'm well versed in the barriers that today's society puts in the way of spending time out of doors with children. Richard Louv in his book *Last Child in the Woods: Saving Our Children from Nature-Deficit Disorder* argues that sensationalist media coverage and paranoid parents have scared children away from woods and fields. In my opinion, the opportunity for getting out and doing the wild stuff has to be realistic and local. After-school sports expend energy—and this is important in a world where too many children are clinically obese—but it's not the same as natural, unstructured, out-of-doors play. Our world is filled with stranger-danger rules, which purport to make a child safe. My siblings and I were allowed to take risks, enjoying a freedom that often presented the unexpected such as a bull in a field. The rules of nature's playground are unstructured and yet call for immediacy and sensibility. Solitude is free and sometimes necessary for a naturalist. It is, however, often lacking in a world of sleep-deprived teenagers keeping up with the demands of social media.

Edward O. Wilson's *Biophilia* suggests we need an association with nature in ways we don't fully understand. Encouraging a child to tree hug may not be such a bad idea if we believe that patients who can see green fields recover more quickly than those in a sterile white room. A trip to an arboretum is even more worthwhile if it's a family event. Technology and the virtual world are, however, useful: identifying flora and fauna can be "app fast," while a digital camera leaves no damaging footprints and captures the moment

instantly. The Internet may inform children about Amazon rain-forests but we have to ensure that a child knows the difference between a spider's web and the worldwide one. A child should also know that an Internet spider is not of the Araneae order and that a fine silk web is made from a protein fiber known as gossamer.

Young children are easily persuaded to "come outside." Kicking leaves, splashing in puddles, and cooking with foraged ingredients are all tempting. Older children—or those who are not outdoor types—may need coaxing. Rather than doing chores, carers may also benefit from daily interaction with nature and a teen. Try a 5-minute excursion into the garden to identify the birds or a walk to spot different plants and flowers. Outdoor friendships will grow as you share thoughts about the natural world.

BioBlitzing is the new craze on the environmental block. Blitzing anything demands caution, but this idea enthuses about biodiversity by concentrating on one area and "blitzing" all the wildlife—in the sense of finding, identifying, and recording. For those who aren't team members, the dawn chorus society can run barefoot in the dew, while the owl appreciation society might count moths before bed. Unlike clubs, nature doesn't time-keep, except on the beach where you need to watch the tide.

IMPORTANT NOTE FOR CARERS
When working on projects, children should be supervised and helped where necessary, especially when using penknives and other sharp implements.

A Basic Wild Knapsack

Here is a list of useful items for wild adventures. Before you set off, think about the type of environment you're visiting and take all the things you may need, so you can get the most out of your wild experience.

* Bottle of water

* Scissors

* Penknife

* Hand pruners/ secateurs (older children)

* Double-sided tape

* String and thread

* Magnifying glass

* Pocket-sized I.D. book

* First aid kit (including band-aids, antiseptic wipes, and insect repellent)

* Cellphone/mobile phone (for useful apps and safety)

* Camera

* Snap-and-seal bags

* Small plastic containers with lids (a short-stay bug home—you can never have too many of these)

* Small wind-up flashlight/torch (for looking into cracks and rock-pooling)

* Notepad (make a habit of writing up your discoveries)

* Pencil (this won't blot if it gets wet)

* Small paintbrush

* Old spoon

* Small sieve

* Bucket (for pond dipping and rock-pooling)

* Tape measure

* Tweezers

* Bin liner (make a head hole for a waterproof or use it for any garbage)

* *Summer* Sunscreen and sun hat

* *Winter* Warm hat and washable gloves

Not Fur or Feather but Some Clothing Thoughts

Wear the right clothes for the habitat you're exploring and pack to keep yourself safe. Here are some tips:

* Make sure you have a warm sweater and a wrap-away waterproof jacket.

* A lightweight buff is really useful because it can be used as a hat as well as a neck warmer.

* If it's hot, keep out of the midday sun and wear cotton clothing to stay as cool as possible.

* Wear layers—it is much better to be too warm than too cold. Layers can be peeled off.

* A wetsuit is useful if you're spending time in wetlands or by the seashore.

* Dress: camouflage yourself and choose nature's colors. Greens and browns, not neon red, are nature's choices.

* Wear strong and suitable footwear.

Young Naturalist Extras

Being a naturalist is not expensive. Nature is there for everyone to enjoy—there isn't an entry charge. If, however, you enjoy looking at plants and wildlife, and cooking with wild ingredients, you may find this list of additional items helpful:

* Waterproof camera (although expensive, a photograph captures plants, seaweed, and wildlife without disturbing the environment)

* Waterproof binoculars

* Telescope

* Microscope

* Food dehydrator (for drying blossom, leaves, berries, and seaweed)

* Digital scales for accurately weighing seaweed, petals, and other dried ingredients (dried ingredients are light in weight)

* Blotting paper

* Scrapbooks

Young Naturalists

A naturalist is a person who studies the world of nature. Naturalists are often interested in botany, geology, animals, marine life, and the environment—a really broad range of subjects. A list of important naturalists would be long, but you might like to read more about Charles Darwin, Thomas Jefferson, and Henry Thoreau, who all believed that it was important to conserve the environment for future generations.

SOME FAMOUS NATURALISTS

Botany was a passion for many 19th-century people and the study of nature was a popular pastime. However, until the mid-19th century, girls couldn't study at university, although many women enjoyed being outdoors and learning about the natural world. Margaret Gatty and Mary Brewster, for example, were 19th-century ladies who collected seaweed specimens and worked with male professors. In the United Kingdom, Margaret Gatty wrote books about seaweed and nature, and involved her children too. She also wrote stories for children that link religion and the natural world. At the same time, in North America, Mary Brewster collected seaweed and corresponded with Professor William Setchell at U.C. Berkeley. Similarly, Beatrix Potter (1866–1943) loved nature and was interested in every branch of natural science except astronomy. As was common in the Victorian era, women of Potter's class were often educated at home and rarely went to university. Beatrix Potter's parents did not, however, discourage her enquiring mind and she spent lots of time in her local London museums. Potter was primarily an author, but also helped to discover Buller's drops (see page 43).

My Side of the Mountain, a book by Jean Craighead George, has made lots of American children aware of the diversity of nature and the value of human contact with wild animals. George researched her books through her own observations and also wrote a collection of wild recipes for children. Another plant-lover who recognized the importance of plants was the poet

Samuel Taylor Coleridge (1772–1834). He wrote: *"Plants exist in themselves. Insects by, or by means of, themselves. Men for themselves. There is a growth only in plants."* Humans are a part of life but we have to understand nature and work with it. Indeed, in 1802 Coleridge wrote: *"Everything has a life of its own… and that we are all one life."* Later in this section, you can read how important flowers are for pollinators (see page 17) and also how plants purify our air and fight against climate change (see page 18). In the 19th century, flowers were given random, non-scientific meanings, which you can read about in Kate Greenaway's *Language of Flowers* and Cecily Mary Barker's *Flower Fairy* series. Whatever your thoughts on flower language and fairies, the plant kingdom is clearly very important.

CHARLES DARWIN The 19th century was a time of huge expansion in our understanding of natural science. On the back of the manuscript for his book *On the Origin of Species* (1859), Darwin's son Francis doodled "the battle of the fruit and vegetable soldiers." On another of

Darwin's papers, a child has drawn birds catching a spider and an insect. Darwin certainly involved his children in his passion for studying wildlife. The flowers and butterflies drawn by his children are very detailed. Darwin's famous sand-walk or "thinking path" was where he thought about his theory of evolution. He strolled there every morning and afternoon with Polly, his white fox terrier, while his children played among the trees and bushes. Darwin's son Francis later wrote: "*The Sand-walk was our play-ground as children, and here we continually saw my father as he walked round. He liked to see what we were doing, and was ever ready to sympathize in any fun that was going on.*" Getting involved with nature requires setting aside time, but families can do this together—just as the Darwin family did.

JOHN MUIR Another naturalist of influence, John Muir was born in Scotland but emigrated to North America, where he is sometimes called "The Father of the National Parks." He left Wisconsin University to attend what he called *The University of Wilderness*. Muir is quoted as having said, "Any fool can destroy trees, they can't run away." Sometimes we need people to say things like this to make us stop and think. The preservationist John Muir and the conservationist Gifford Pinchot had heated discussions. There is a natural tension between those who want to

A Forward-thinking President

Presidents can be conservationists too. Theodore Roosevelt once said, "There can be no greater issue than that of conservation in this country. Just as we must conserve our men, women, and children, so we must conserve the resources of the land on which they live."

Nature table

preserve nature and those who care about their natural environment, but harvest food and cut wood to help society. Muir and Pinchot had disagreements about public land, but they often worked on projects together. On a joint expedition to the Grand Canyon, they spotted a tarantula. When Pinchot raised his boot to step on the creature, Muir told him that the tarantula had just as much right to be on the trail as they did. Muir did not want to destroy nature, whereas Pinchot, although very fond of nature, was happy to intervene if he thought it would make things better.

SIR DAVID ATTENBOROUGH is a contemporary British naturalist and wildlife presenter. He is often asked the question, "How did you become interested in animals?" His response is always the same, "How on earth did you lose interest in them?" When David Attenborough was invited to the White House, he told President Barack Obama how important it is for children to understand the natural world. He said: "This is the only planet we've got and we've got to protect it."

THE FIRST ECOLOGIST

The first ecologist is considered to be Gilbert White, author of *The Natural History of Selborne*. His book, written in 1789, is a collection of letters written to his friends, the zoologist Thomas Pennant and the explorer and naturalist Daines Barrington. Gilbert White lived in Selborne, in Hampshire, England, where he wrote about living birds and animals in their natural habitat. This was unusual because most 18th-century naturalists studied dead specimens. His book was written in a chatty style, at a time when many science books were written in Latin and natural history was regarded as folklore (tradition passed down by word-of-mouth). The word folklore was first used in 1846, a time when there was a rush of scientific progress by naturalists.

Gilbert White was lucky because he had time to write to his friends and patiently watch wildlife. He not only discovered the harvest mouse (*Micromys minutus*) and noctule bat (*Nyctalus noctula*), but also distinguished between the chiffchaff (*Phylloscopus collybita*), willow warbler (*Phylloscopus trochilus*), and wood warbler (*Phylloscopus sibilatrix*). By listening to the birds' songs and spotting tiny differences in their plumage, Gilbert White identified three different birds. Before this, they were all called a willow wren. If you are interested in birds, find out more about the Audubon Society, which is named after the great ornithologist John Audubon, the author of *Birds of America*. In the United Kingdom, The Royal Society for the Protection of Birds (RSPB) has local groups and interesting resources to help you learn more about birds.

Classifying Plants and Animals

Grouping living things together by their similarities is not always easy, but it shows how one is related to another. Carolus Linnaeus (1707–1778) is known as the "Father of Systematic Botany" for doing just this by adopting a two-word (binomial) system using Latin names—the natural scientist Gilbert White used this system. Linnaeus' system (or taxonomy) has seven levels of classification as follows: Kingdom, Division (plants and fungi)/Phylum (animals), Class, Order, Family, Genus, and, finally, Species (see below left). The diagram below right shows the classification of the United Kingdom red squirrel (*Sciurus vulgaris*).

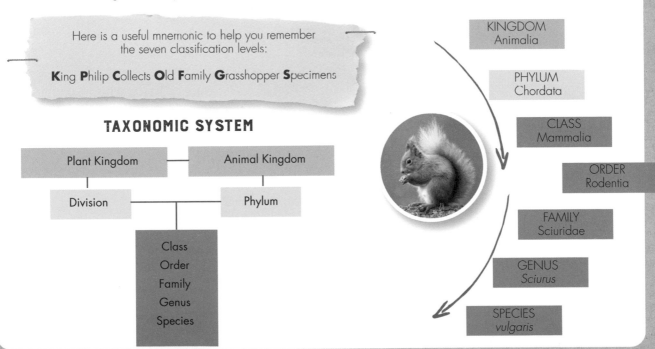

Here is a useful mnemonic to help you remember the seven classification levels:

King **P**hilip **C**ollects **O**ld **F**amily **G**rasshopper **S**pecimens

TAXONOMIC SYSTEM

Plant Kingdom — Animal Kingdom

Division — Phylum

Class
Order
Family
Genus
Species

KINGDOM
Animalia

PHYLUM
Chordata

CLASS
Mammalia

ORDER
Rodentia

FAMILY
Sciuridae

GENUS
Sciurus

SPECIES
vulgaris

BE A PIONEERING NATURALIST If you want to become a naturalist, then it's helpful to emulate other naturalists such as Gilbert White and John Lewis-Stempel. Stempel is a contemporary British naturalist and author who is often outdoors. He probably doesn't notice a few drops of rain, the wind, or the dampness of the ditch he is crouching in because he is watching flora and fauna. Here are some helpful tips for becoming a naturalist:

* Naturalists are quiet and move stealthily, if at all. You need to be sharp-eared and eagle-eyed to learn first-hand about the natural world.

* Move when the wind rustles the leaves. Stop or move stealthily when the wind drops.

* Blend in and take advantage of natural cover.

* Avoid being down wind of an animal. Human scent travels. Wild teens should leave aftershave and perfume at home. Try to walk into the breeze to avoid sharing your scent with wildlife.

BEING IN TUNE WITH NATURE

Our forefathers were in touch with the rhythm of the seasons, but modern life has sadly cut us off from such close contact with nature. An understanding of our natural world links you closely with your grandparents and generations before them. This doesn't mean young naturalists can't be techie too, though. Digital cameras are amazing; they can be used to capture wild plants and animals in an instant. Geocaching is a modern treasure hunt activity that uses GPS (Global Positioning System). Seekers are directed toward small stashes of treasure in urban and rural spots. Once there, the geocachers record the visit in the log book (or online) and take and replace small trinkets of treasure. On another day you might want to spend time in the wild on your own and simply be still and quiet (see *The Sound of Wild Silence*, opposite).

Observing Plants and Animals

In Romans times a vivarium was an indoor enclosure for looking at flora and fauna. *Vivarium* comes from the Latin "to live." If you keep a pet in a hutch or build a house in the wild for a hibernating hedgehog, you could call this a vivarium. Fish are kept in an aquarium and you study salt-based animal life in a marine aquarium. The first aquarium was probably kept by Anne Thynne (1806–1866), who studied seaweeds and stony corals. More recently, aquariums have been made into coffee tables and even an Apple Mac computer. A terrarium is like an aquarium but used to house plants, although some people keep reptiles in them. It was invented in 1833 by Doctor Nathaniel Bagshaw Ward who was interested in ferns. (To learn more about ferns, see page 29.)

The Sound of Wild Silence

Go out into the wild: sit down, listen, watch, smell the air, and be still. Sense the seasons. Write down what you see, smell, and hear. Tap your head and become yourself again.

Helpful Plants

* **Stinging nettles** (*Urtica dioica*) If you're stung by a stinging nettle, nature has the antidote—look for a dock leaf (*Rumex patientia*) and rub it on the rash. Some older people say that nettles help arthritis and so they don't mind brushing against stinging nettles.

* **Ribwort plantain** (*Plantago lanceolata*) This plant was carried by soldiers into battle and used to treat wounds on the battlefield. This is why it is sometimes called soldier's herb. Native Americans called the plant white man's footprint because it appeared with European settlers. They did, however, know of its healing value because they also called it "life medicine." The leaves were mashed to reduce bleeding and to draw out thorns and splinters—you could try this out.

* The Ancient Greeks used seaweed to treat swollen glands, but Italian physicians of the School of Salerno were the first to use seaweed to treat goitre (an enlarged thyroid). Seaweed has traditionally been used in many cultures to heal wounds. Today, hospitals use seaweed in some wound dressings.

Be Safe and Mindful in the Countryside

Here are some things to think about when you're having fun outdoors.

☞ Always ask an adult to go to wild places with you.

☞ I.D. is the wild kids' code word for identification. Don't pick or eat anything unless you are absolutely sure you know what it is.

☞ Cooking poisonous plants does not make them safe.

☞ Always wash your hands after handling things in the wild and especially well after touching bones and animal droppings.

☞ Don't pick plants that are protected by government law (see *Conservation Matters*, on page 17).

☞ Don't pull up plant roots.

☞ When foraging, don't be greedy—pick a little here and there.

☞ Pick wild salad leaves slowly and I.D. each leaf with care, ensuring you don't pick different species that may be growing nearby.

☞ Be alert to fire, snakes, and ticks. Ticks are a nuisance and can cause Lyme disease.

☞ Keep pets under control and respect livestock. Keep your distance from cattle with calves.

☞ Keep to paths when asked to do so and shut gates. Don't damage hedges, walls, or fences.

☞ Care for the countryside—leave no more than a footprint.

Plants to I.D. and Avoid

Nature provides free food and medicines, but we need to learn how to I.D. plants correctly. Each of us has different tolerances when we touch plants and the contact time for a bad reaction can vary from person to person. Young naturalists must learn about harmful as well as edible plants. Make a list of poisonous plants to look out for in your neighborhood. Your local environmental agency will give you helpful advice.

WILD POISONS

- Castor bean plant (*Ricinus communis*)

- Deadly nightshade (*Atropa belladonna*) If you eat the leaves and/or berries of this plant, you can die. This is why it is called deadly.

- Foxgloves (*Digitalis* spp.) If you know someone with a heart condition, you may recognize this plant's Latin name because the leaves are used in the heart drug digitalis. Although some poisonous plants are used in medicines, this does not mean that you can eat them.

- Hemlock (*Conium maculatum*) The philosopher Socrates was given a cup of poisonous hemlock juice to drink after his trial—he died. This is a plant to learn to I.D. and then avoid.

- The red berries of Jack in the pulpit (*Arum maculatum*)—also known as cuckoo pint or lords and ladies—are pretty but poisonous. This plant sometimes grows near wild garlic, so make sure you don't pick a handful in error. All parts are toxic.

- Mistletoe (*Phoradendron*/USA and *Viscum album*/UK); American poison ivy (*Toxicodendron* spp.); British ivy (*Hedera helix*); and yew (*Taxus baccata*) are all poisonous. Yew is one of the deadliest trees in the world. The berries and leaves of some of these plants are used for Christmas decorations and, although birds enjoy eating these berries, humans must not. Always wash your hands after touching any flora or fauna.

OTHER PLANTS TO LOOK OUT FOR

- Giant hogweed (*Heracleum sphondylium*) can grow to enormous heights—much taller than an adult. If its sap comes in contact with your skin, it can burn and leave horrid blisters.

- Be wary of bushes with thorns and trees with needles. Thorns from wild roses and blackberry bushes, as well as sharp pine needles, can cause infection if they aren't removed quickly.

- Avoid ragwort (*Jacobaea vulgaris*) if you suffer from allergies or asthma. It is poisonous to horses. Scots call ragwort stinking Willie after William Duke of Cumberland who led the loyalists at the Battle of Culloden against Bonnie Prince Charlie and the Jacobites—the battle path was covered with ragwort.

UNLUCKY PLANTS

- Blackthorn (*Prunus spinosa*) Country people refused to bring blackthorn into the house as it was considered a bad omen—usually indicating that somebody would die.

- Holly (*Ilex aquifolium*) It was said to be unlucky to hang this evergreen over mirrors at Christmas.

- Mistletoe It was thought unlucky to bring mistletoe indoors before Christmas Eve.

- All decorations, including holly and mistletoe, had to be taken down before Old Christmas Day (or Twelfth Night)—or it was believed that the "Devil would dance on every spray."

DON'T MUNCH ON A HUNCH

If you go mushrooming—or 'shrooming as some people call it—you should only pick a specimen if you are 100 percent sure you have identified it correctly. Eating the wrong wild food can be very dangerous. Mushroom poisoning has a long history—in Ancient Rome the Emperor Claudius was fed poisonous mushrooms by his wife Agrippina because she wanted her son Nero to become emperor. Cooking doesn't kill fungi toxicity. Just because an animal finds a fungus moreish does not guarantee it is also safe for you to eat. Dodgy mushrooms are in the minority, but the scary stats are there—it only takes one mistake, so be careful and remember:

If you are in any I.D. doubt, leave a mushroom out of your foraging basket.

Seasons and Weather

In the fall (autumn), nature's carpet is soft and leafy. In winter the ground hardens and there is sometimes snow—deer are forced to eat dead leaves or tree bark and lichen. Reindeer like eating a lichen called reindeer moss (*Cladonia rangiferina*). In dry weather this silvery-gray lichen crumbles underfoot but when soaked by rain, it bounces.

THE SEASONAL CYCLE

As the seasons unfold, there are many changes to see in the natural world, as well as special festivals to celebrate.

SPRING New leaves appear in spring and winter-hibernating animals sniff the air to see if it's warm enough to wake up. A new generation of wildlife is born. The warming sun encourages plant life and food becomes more plentiful after the winter famine. Birds lay eggs, migrating birds return, and Christians look forward to Easter; it's all about birth. In the Northern Hemisphere, May Day is roughly midway between the spring equinox and summer solstice (the longest day of the year). Beltane, an ancient Celtic May Day festival, celebrated the beginning of summer. Cattle were driven out to grass pastures and there was feasting, dancing, and singing. Lots of traditional May Day celebrations involved a colorfully decorated small tree, bush, or pole. Folklorists have recorded many seasonal flower and plant traditions, which you can learn more about if you're interested. Snowdrops (*Galanthus* spp.), for example, are sometimes called Candlemas bells because big bunches were picked to decorate chapels on Candlemas Day (February 1).

SUMMER Flying insects are attracted to summer flowers by their blossom juice. These insects help plants to reproduce by brushing on pollen dust as they guzzle nectar and then transferring the pollen to the next flower. Nectar is a mixture of sugars and water—an energy drink for insects. It's a reward for the work they do gathering pollen and pollinating flowers (see *What is Pollination?*, on page 51). Pollen floating in the air may make you sneeze, but clever insects carry it from plant to plant. Summer is a busy time of year.

FALL This is when the leaves of deciduous trees color and fall, and ferns turn brown. Late summer and early fall are also when wildlife gathers food while it is plentiful. The expression to "squirrel things away" comes from the squirrel. They are hoarders. Squirrels are smart: they can tell if a nut is rotten without opening it. They also have very good memories and hide nuts that they can come back to when food is scarce. A red squirrel can find food buried under several meters of snow. Meanwhile, some species of birds migrate on long flights to warmer climates.

WINTER This is when the countryside appears to sleep, with deciduous trees ceasing to photosynthesize (see page 37) and many creatures such as hedgehogs going into hibernation. At this time of year, however, you will find star- and moon-gazing (see page 142–44) much more fun because hours of darkness are longer. Also, if you go tracking after a snowfall, wildlife tracks will be very clear (see page 122). This is a good tip to pass on to a novice naturalist.

WHATEVER THE WEATHER

Keen naturalists cope, whether it's hot, raining, or snowing. It's not a question of bad weather, but being badly dressed for the weather conditions. Seasoned wild kids know that it's easier to take off a sweater and tie it around their waist than to suffer from chattering teeth and goose pimples. Fishermen and farmers plan their livelihoods according to the weather forecast and people called storm-chasers seek out wild weather so they can experience it. Some of these chasers are scientists who want to find out what causes storms. You could become a local weather watcher. Keep a daily weather record: measure rainfall in a glass jar in the garden and take photographs of cloudscapes.

WINDY WEATHER The Beaufort Scale is used throughout the marine world to measure wind speed. Wind drives the weather machine. It pushes along clouds and brings rain, and weather systems are produced when hot and cold air meet. Sinking air creates an area of high pressure and clear blue skies, and this makes people feel happy. Low pressure often means that the sky is sheeted with cloud. A cloud is a large collection of water droplets or ice crystals. Understanding clouds is useful because they express the weather's mood. You can use clouds to accurately forecast the weather for the next hour or so—this is helpful when you're exploring the wild. Cloud names have their roots in Latin. *Cumulus* (from the Latin word for "heaped") clouds are lumpy and often look like cauliflowers. *Alto* means "high"; *altocumulus* clouds are high cumulus clouds. *Cirrus* (Latin for "curl" or "fringe") clouds are made of ice crystals and occur when it's cold. Other useful words to understand are *nimbus* (which means "precipitation" or "rain") and *stratus* (meaning "layer"). *Stratus* clouds are low and gray. If snow or rain falls, the clouds are called *nimbostratus*. Visit the website www.cloudappreciationsociety.org to learn more about cloud-spotting. Cloud names may confuse you to begin with, but just remember that the higher the clouds, the better the weather will be.

LET IT SNOW Snow is frozen water crystals. Snow looks white because it reflects most of the visible light that strikes it. In very cold weather, snow is dust-like; when the temperature is a little higher, the flakes are bigger and wetter. Pliny, the Roman author and naturalist, and Benedict de Saussure, the 18th-century alpinist, both describe red snow. Sometimes this is called watermelon snow. It is caused by the freshwater algae *Chlamydomonas nivalis* which contains a red coloring. Red snow is most common in coastal polar regions and alpine areas. Playing in the snow is fun, but using snow to build an emergency shelter in winter is an important survival skill. Snow houses trap warm air because the snow acts as an insulator. An igloo is a well-built snow house and provides a very effective barrier against wind chill, which makes us feel cold.

NATURAL FORECASTERS

The tiny scarlet pimpernel (*Anagallis arvensis*) is a common cornfield and garden weed. The flower is usually a striking scarlet and doesn't open in bad weather. It is sometimes called poor man's weather glass or barometer. Some botanists suggest its petals open at 8:00am and close again at 3:00pm, but wild flowers keep summer daylight, not shopkeeper, hours. You might like to make a timesheet for this flower and see if it opens and shuts its petals like clockwork. Create your own list of fair-weather flowers and look at the scales on cones too. These open in sunshine and close when it's damp. Seaweeds such as sugar kelp can also be used as natural forecasters (see page 82).

Scarlet pimpernel

Sugar kelp

Conservation Matters

Healthy people eat a balanced diet. There is also a food balance between plants and animals living close to each other. Plant-eating animals are called herbivores and carnivores eat these plant-eaters. Omnivores aren't fussy: they eat plants and animals. Nature provides balanced ecosystems. Human activity can, however, unsettle this balance. Forestry, intensive farming, fishing, global warming, and industrial pollution can all affect nature's rhythm.

OUR CHANGING LANDSCAPE

Until recently, some farmers sowed and grazed the land that was once hedgerow to keep up with our increasing demand for food. Meanwhile, wetlands are drained and crops sprayed with fertilizers. These methods of intensive farming, teamed with the use of pesticides, leave little room for the wild flowers that are essential for pollinating insects. It is only recently that we have thought very much about the effect our lifestyles and farming choices have on the environment. We must be careful that our farming and fishing methods don't make wildlife and plants disappear—like the dinosaurs. This is why we have countryside rules, must try to conserve habitats, and list flora and fauna that need protection.

ENCOURAGING BIODIVERSITY Over the last 50 years, landscapes have changed in Europe and North America. This is why countries now think about sustainable land management—we need biodiversity (different types of life). New hedges are being planted and field edges aren't sown for cropping. This allows wild flowers to grow at the boundaries of fields. You too could sow wild flower seeds to encourage insects to visit.

PROTECTING THE POLLINATORS Many of the crops we eat, as well as the majority of wild plants, are pollinated by bees and hoverflies. In fact, bees are thought to be responsible for the pollination of about one third of the world's food. Butterflies, moths, and other flying insects are also important. Sadly, one third of European

butterflies are in decline and more than 60 moth species have become extinct in the UK since 1900. Some fruits depend on insect pollination. This is a free ecosystem; humans don't need to do anything. However, unless the decline in bees and other pollinators is halted, farmers may have to rely on hand-pollination. This would be very time-consuming and make food more expensive. Increasingly, humans are finding that they need to help nature out. For instance, farmers in the Chinese province of Sichuan use chicken-feather brushes to pollinate apple flowers.

European peacock butterfly (*Aglais io*)

Research by Professor Memmott at the University of Bristol, in England, suggests that strawberries are bigger when pollinated by bees that have fed on wild flowers. City and garden flowers can also support large numbers of pollinators. You can help out here by not mowing the verges by your driveway—wild flowers like growing here. Pollinators supply a very important ecological service and are vital to our food chain.

BAT CONSERVATION ALERT Bats, which are the only mammals capable of powered flight, are often associated with Hallowe'en, but since 2006 more than a million bats have died from a fungal disease called White-Nose Syndrome. Bats are useful mammals because they eat insects and this reduces harm to crops. This means that farmers can use fewer pesticides. According to researchers, a single colony of 150 big brown bats

Bat poo

(*Eptesicus fuscus*) in Indiana eats nearly 1.3 million insects a year. Bats are nature's way of helping the farmer out. It means the farmer doesn't need to purchase expensive pesticides, which adds to the cost of our food. All bats are protected by law in the United Kingdom and by federal and state laws in North America. If you see this nocturnal mammal fluttering at dusk, or look at bat poo through a magnifying glass, remember: bats are valuable to our environment and not just for Hallowe'en.

GLOBAL WARMING

A glasshouse is always warm. The glass allows the sun's rays to shine in, but prevents the heat escaping. The gases on Earth act like the glass in a glasshouse. The Earth is warmed by the sun, but its gases (known as greenhouse gases) prevent heat escaping—they trap the sun's energy. The warming of Earth is called the greenhouse effect. The Earth's atmosphere contains these gases naturally but, over the last 20 years or so, increasing carbon dioxide levels have pushed up greenhouse gases to record highs. This has caused the temperature of the Earth to increase.

Although plants and oceans both absorb carbon dioxide, they can't keep up with the extra quantities that are being pumped into the atmosphere. This build-up of carbon dioxide causes global warming. Scientists believe this is due to human activities. Without the greenhouse effect the Earth would be too cold for humans to live. If the greenhouse effect becomes stronger, it will affect the careful balance between humans, plants, and animals. Some species are already responding to warmer climates by moving to cooler areas (such as the red squirrel in the United Kingdom and North America). We may also see plants blossoming earlier and lasting longer into the fall (autumn), and animal hibernation and bird migration times changing too. *Climate change alters the life cycles of plants and animals.*

The Fungal Internet

Mycorrhiza describes the "give-and-take" relationship between fungi and plants. Plants provide fungi with food, while fungi help plants suck up water and grab nutrients via mycelia (see page 42). Carbohydrates, nutrients, and water are distributed in a sort of underground plumbing system. These mycorrhizal networks are sometimes described as the Earth's Natural Internet or the Wood Wide Web. Scientists are researching these underground secrets. As they do, they are also learning about a dark side of the Fungal Internet, where nutrients are hijacked, rather than the plants and fungi mutually helping each other out.

Several species of fungi belong to the *Armillaria* genus, which is popularly known as honey fungus. One species, which grows in the Blue Mountains in Oregon, spans 2,384 acres and is estimated to be over 2,400 years old—although we have only just become aware of its existence. It is the world's largest organism and could be older, giving it a place among the oldest living things on Earth. This honey fungus grabs good nutrients from host (trees) but gives nothing back, and so the trees become weak. The fungus grows using tube-like forms called hypha that branch out like a motorway network, connecting multiple tree roots. It's a sinister tale. Ash dieback is a similar United Kingdom story. A greedy fungus called *Hymenoscyphus fraxineus* thrives, while the ash tree's leaves go black until it eventually "dies back" from the top. The fungus takes its food and gives nothing back to the ash—it's a one-way freeway.

Be a Citizen Naturalist

When you go for a walk in the woods, look for signs of disease and report this back to those that collect information on your nation's trees. Scientists can't be everywhere and, as a citizen naturalist, you can help by being on tree alert. From a practical point-of-view, if you spot diseased trees, clean the mud from your boots before you leave the woods. This will stop the disease spreading.

Humans breathe in oxygen and breathe out carbon dioxide, and trees do the opposite (see *What is Photosynthesis?*, on page 37) and so help to balance the level of gases in the air. Nature is clever.

NATIVE VERSUS NON-NATIVE SPECIES

Native species are those plants and animals that have evolved over time to thrive in a particular habitat. Non-native species are plants and animals that have found their way to a new habitat through human activity. Some non-native species can become invasive, damaging or displacing native species, which can be harmful to the environment.

A TALE OF TWO SQUIRRELS Gray squirrels burying hazelnuts and acorns are a familiar sight in the fall (autumn), but the red squirrel (*Tamiasciurus hudsonicus*/USA and *Sciurus vulgaris*/UK) used to be more common in the United States and United Kingdom than they are today. One reason for this is that squirrels prefer conifer and mixed woodland, but have had to move north as these habitats have been destroyed. Unlike humans, squirrels aren't able to react quickly to change.

The North American gray squirrel (*Sciurus carolinensis*) was introduced to the United Kingdom in the mid-19th century and is now more common than the native red squirrel. The non-native gray is considered to be an invasive species and is blamed for the decline in the number of red squirrels. Habitat loss is, however, probably the main reason for this. Although grays do not kill reds, they do spread a nasty disease called squirrelpox (to which they are immune) that kills red squirrels.

In the past, red squirrels were seen as pests and killed—children would shoot them with catapults. In the UK, pine martens (*Martes martes*) were also hunted for fur and predator control. It is a good idea to be able to I.D. pine marten tracks because this cat-sized animal, which is a relative of badgers and weasels, is now rare.

MARINE INVASIVES There are marine as well as terrestrial invasive species. Signal crayfish (*Pacifastacus leniusculus*) are native to North America and were introduced to Europe in the 1960s. The signal crayfish is encased in a tough shell and armed with two large pincers. It spreads a disease called crayfish plague. This aggressive species is at home on land, too, and can walk for several miles across country in search of new territory. When signal crayfish move into a stretch of river, it's bad news for the native white-clawed crayfish (*Austropotamobius pallipes*), which is now classified as endangered. Marine biologists are looking for a way to halt the spread of signal crayfish. The rusty crayfish (*Orconectes rusticus*), which is native to the Ohio River Basin, is causing a similar problem in Ontario, Canada. If you learn to I.D. invasive species, you can help to prevent their spread by reporting the sighting to an environmental agency. Remember that invasive species threaten the fragile balance of ecosystems.

Reducing Your Carbon and Beach Footprint

Here are some tips to help you reduce the impact you have on the environment on a day-to-day basis:

* Save energy—every little saving helps, so cover saucepans as you cook, switch off electrical equipment, and turn off lights as you leave a room.

* Save water—by turning off the water as you brush your teeth and taking showers instead of baths.

* Use cold (not hot) water to wash your hands after going to the lavatory.

* Close doors to keep in heat.

* Don't be a litterbug and think about joining a beach or land litter clear-up.

* Think conservation before you release a plastic balloon into the sky or throw a plastic bottle into fresh or sea water.

* Clever naturalists don't shout because this frightens wildlife away. Simple thoughtful action can make a HUGE environmental difference.

NOTE: Some animals (including marine life) are vulnerable and some plants are becoming rare. As a result, many species are protected by state and federal wildlife laws. Make a list of protected flora and fauna species local to you. You could also ask your local environment agency about the administration and regulation of nature conservation and wildlife.

Our Precious Oceans

Oceans absorb carbon-dioxide pollution, as well as heat resulting from the greenhouse effect. Worryingly oceans are getting warmer, while sea levels are rising as the ice caps melt and this threatens the foundations of life in the oceans.

SAVE OUR SEAS

As weather patterns change, vital habitats such as coral reefs are being lost. Coral reefs are created in shallow tropical waters by tiny animals called corals. Each coral makes a skeleton for itself, and these skeletons build up over time to create coral reefs. The reefs provide shelter for sea life. Warmer water has, however, damaged coral reefs in many parts of the world. The loss of a coral-reef ecosystem is important because it reduces habitats for sea creatures, such as lobsters and conch, and disrupts the food web that connects ocean life. Coral reefs also help humans out because they break the force of strong waves and storms before they reach the seashore.

OCEAN POLLUTION is another environmental problem. For a long time, people thought getting rid of waste at sea was a good idea, but it isn't. When you're trying to reduce your carbon footprint on land, think about the fun of running barefoot on a clean, sandy beach. Today, thousands of flip-flops are washed up on beaches of the East African coast. This manmade garbage spoils the seashore and also messes up the fragile ocean ecosystem. A company called *Ocean Sole* transforms discarded plastic sandals into art. This provides jobs for local people, cleans up beaches, and makes people think about marine conservation when they see the flip-flop artwork. *Ocean Sole* is a cool name for a company and a clever way of cleaning up pollution.

Homeless hermit crabs shelter in secondhand shells to protect their soft shells from predators but, nowadays, they make homes in human plastic waste—perhaps a toothpaste cap. Some sea life has, however, died after swallowing plastic which they mistook for jellyfish. Mermaid tears or nurdles (plastic pellets) are easily mistaken for food and, as yet, we don't know if fish that have eaten plastic can harm us. Birds eat plastic meals too when they misidentify nurdles for fish eggs—the real meal. We need to save our seas from plastic pollution. The hermit crab may have chosen to house itself in plastic, but humans must not fill their environment with garbage.

FISHY FOOD FOR THOUGHT

Countries around the world rely on wild fish to provide food and employment within the marine industry, but our demand for fish has led to fishing practices that are depleting fish and shellfish populations. We are taking too many fish from our seas. A conservationist plans ahead and purchases fish that is from a sustainable species. Policymakers estimate the percentage of fish that can be fished without harm by counting the number of juvenile fish. To maintain a healthy population, the number of young fish must exceed the number of fish taken from the sea. One way to learn about fish is to go sea or freshwater fishing. Fish sustainably. Join the fishermen, and throw fish back into the river or sea after you have had a good look at them.

GHOST FISHING This term describes what happens when old fishing equipment is dumped in the sea. Not only can this harm scuba divers, but abandoned nets or lost fishing gear also trap sea animals and may kill marine life. Divers are now on a global healthy seas mission to remove marine litter from the bottom of the sea. They have exciting recycling projects that you may like to find out about.

Oily Feathers

Animals with feathers are called birds. There are two types of feathers: contour feathers and down feathers. Contour feathers protect birds from wind and water. You'll often see birds preening their feathers to keep them clean and in line. Larger contour flight feathers help support a bird's weight as it flies. Under the contour feathers are down feathers, which keep birds warm. An oil spillage from a tanker at sea causes terrible damage to seabirds and other wildlife. If the seabirds aren't rescued quickly, thousands of them will die. Have a go at this simple experiment to see what happens to a bird's feathers when they come into contact with oil. Find two contour feathers. Paint cooking oil on one and water on the other using different paintbrushes. The water will remain on the surface of the first feather, while the oil will soak into the second. Birds with oily feathers can't fly or dive and so die from cold and hunger.

Flying with Plastic

This carrier-bag kite doesn't have a frame, so it is quick and simple to make. If you are a good beachcomber, you may even find some abandoned string on the beach or the seaweed dead man's rope (*Chorda filum*). Take a long piece of string or seaweed, tie one end securely to a twig (or a kelp stipe), measuring about 10in (25cm) in length, and wind the string or seaweed neatly around the twig or kelp stipe. Tie the other end of the string or seaweed to the handles of the carrier bag.

Run, catch the wind in the bag, and let the string out as your kite lifts in the wind.

Seagrass Meadows

Seagrasses are grass-like flowering plants (they have roots) with long, ribbon-shaped, dark green leaves. They grow in shallow intertidal and subtidal coastal waters, in sheltered inlets, bays, estuaries, and saltwater lagoons. Seagrasses create one of the world's most widespread habitats, which are sometimes called seagrass (or eelgrass) meadows. Scientists believe that an ancient patch of giant seagrass in the Mediterranean Sea may be one of the oldest living organisms on Earth.

Seagrass meadows are a very important ecosystem, providing essential shelter and food for many species of nursery fish, seahorses, jellyfish, crabs, and other sea life. Sadly, over the last two decades, seagrass habitats have declined. This is due to human activity such as fishing, boat mooring, and coastal development. The good news is that marine conservation zones are being set up to protect further loss of seagrass meadows.

The Kraken

Make this Kraken (or an octopus if you prefer) by recycling a plastic bottle you've found on the beach. It is very easy to make, but adult supervision may be required. Dried pom pom weed (*Vertebrata lanosa*), carrageen (*Chrondus crispus*), or beach sponge are perfect for hair.

WHAT TO USE

- ✔ Scissors
- ✔ 17fl oz (500ml) clean plastic bottle
- ✔ Knife with a pointed end
- ✔ 3 lengths of craft cord, one measuring 28in (70cm) and two measuring ¾–1¼in (2–3cm)
- ✔ Dinner candle in a suitable holder (e.g. a glass bottle)
- ✔ Pair of googly eyes
- ✔ Nail polish
- ✔ Craft glue
- ✔ Dried pom pom weed, carrageen, or sponge (for the hair)
- ✔ 2 pieces of dried dulse or bladder wrack, 6in (15cm) in length

WHAT TO DO

1 Use the scissors to cut the top off the plastic bottle. Turn the bottle upside down and use the pointed knife to make a hole (large enough for threading the craft cord through) in the middle of the bottom of the bottle.

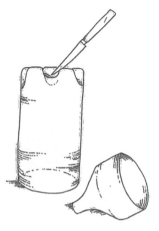

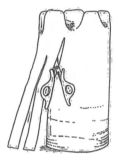

2 Use the scissors to cut strips in the open end of the bottle—these are the Kraken's tentacles—leaving about 1½–2in (4–5cm) of plastic at the base for the Kraken's head. (If you are making an octopus, then you'll need to cut eight tentacle strips.)

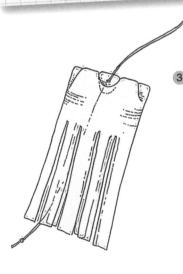

3 Thread the longer piece of craft cord through the hole in the bottom of the bottle (the Kraken's head) and tie a big knot in the end so that you'll be able to hang up your Kraken.

4 Light the candle and then create the wavy tentacles by twisting the strips over the flame to melt the plastic. Be careful, but quick, or the plastic may go black.

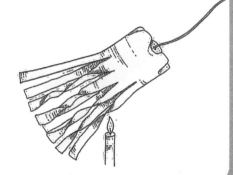

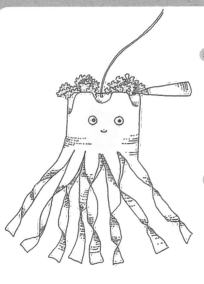

5 Stick on the googly eyes and add extra details with the nail polish.

6 Glue the dried pom pom weed, carrageen, or sponge to the top of the bottle to create the Kraken's hair, and leave to dry.

7 Take the longer piece of craft cord and use the two shorter lengths of cord to tie the pieces of dulse or bladder wrack just above the knot so that the seaweed hangs down the middle of the Kraken. The color of the seaweed will fade over time.

8 Pull the cord through the Kraken's head, taking care not to ruin its hairstyle. Display your Kraken by tying it to a curtain rail or a tree branch in the garden.

Variation

KRAKEN OR OCTOPUS MOBILE

You might like to make a collection of Krakens or octopuses, perhaps using different colored plastic bottles and other species of seaweed.

① Into the Woods

Woods are among the finest natural places to play or find a secret thinking spot. On sunny days, the light flickers and dances through the trees and the leaf canopy is there to protect you if it rains. Sometimes you may not even notice that it's raining. You can explore or play hide-and-seek or tree tag. If you look up, you can spy on squirrels scampering through the trees, while if you look down you can see carpets of winter snowdrops or spring bluebells and white wood sorrel. If you're hungry, you can search for tiny snacks that change with the season—summer brings bilberries and woodland strawberries, while with careful I.D. in the fall (autumn), you can go on a mushroom foray. You might also like to build a woodland den, create a miniature house or garden, go on a woodland bug hunt, or simply play a game of conkers.

The World of Trees

Trees grow nearly everywhere and are fun to climb, hug, or hide behind, but have you ever looked closely at their trunks, branches, and leaves? They are magnificent plants. For example, the bristlecone pines of North America are the longest living trees—some specimens are thought to be over 4,000 years old.

WHAT IS A TREE?

Stand beneath a tree and look up. You'll see an amazing spreading crown of branches and leaves that provides shade for the roots. The branches support the leaves and give the tree its distinctive shape. Tree trunks have evolved to allow trees to tower high above smaller plants so that their leaves can harness energy from the sun to make food, a process known as photosynthesis (see page 37). The underground root system is big because it has to support the tree and also collect water and nutrients from the soil. Root and trunk sizes vary between tree species. As a tree grows, so does its trunk, and this causes the bark to expand. This expansion cracks the bark and helps us to identify different species, as well as young and old trees.

DECIDUOUS TREES

In a broadleaved or deciduous wood (containing trees that shed their leaves), you can name the season simply by looking up at the trees. Just remind yourself of the *False Oats Rhyme* (see page 53). We don't think of trees as having flowers, but they do. In spring and summer you can see and smell the blossom of insect-pollinated trees. The flowers' scent attracts the insects. The pale yellow, scented blossom of the common lime (*Tilia × europaea*)—known as common linden in the United States—is as fragrant as any wild flower. Some pretty catkins, which are tree flowers, even change color. In fall (autumn), a tree's flowers develop into fruits. In contrast, the flowers of wind-pollinated trees don't need to be scented or colorful.

Broadleaved deciduous trees are divided into two groups depending on the shape of the leaf. A leaf is either simple or compound. Most broadleaved trees have simple leaves, which means the leaf is in one piece. A simple leaf may be oval, jagged at the edge, slender, wide, or fanned. The silver birch (*Betula pendula*), for example, has simple, heart-shaped leaves. Interestingly, a fanned leaf may look as though it could come from a compound broadleaved tree but is, in fact, a simple leaf. A compound leaf has two or more leaflets. The rowan or mountain ash (*Sorbus aucuparia*) has compound leaves, which are divided in opposite leaflets.

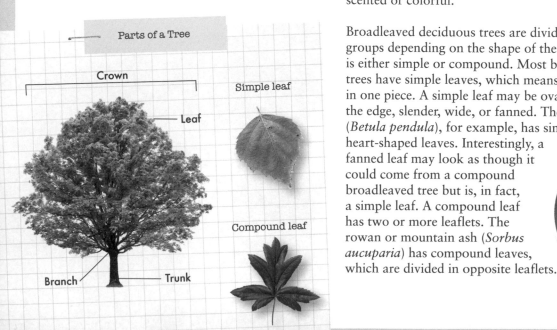

Parts of a Tree

Crown

Simple leaf

Leaf

Compound leaf

Branch

Trunk

Berries on
a rowan tree

EVERGREEN TREES

Evergreen trees have hard leaves called needles or scales (often just described as needles), depending on their shape. Pines (*Pinus* spp.), firs (*Abies* spp.), and spruces (*Picea* spp.) are all needle-leaved evergreens. Needles come in different shapes and sizes. To help I.D. the tree, look at where the needles grow on a twig and how they are grouped. Use a magnifying glass to inspect the needle and see if it's made of scales. You can collect pine and fir needles to make tea (see *Pineapple Weed Tea*, on page 151). Unlike the leaves of deciduous trees, needles are usually long and thin. This helps to slow down water evaporation and means that evergreen trees can grow where other trees can't. The leaves of evergreen trees remain on the tree, but fall off gradually. Many tropical trees keep their leaves all year too. The seeds of most needle-leaved trees grow in woody cones—hence the name conifer. When the cone opens, the seeds fall out (unless they've been nibbled by wildlife).

When you look up at very tall evergreen trees, you'll notice that some of the branches don't start until around 98ft (30m) above the ground—this means that you can walk through a forest of tree trunks. Some of the world's tallest trees are the evergreen coastal redwood (*Sequoia sempervirens*) and the giant redwood (*Sequoiadendron giganteum*). The branches of tall evergreens are a brilliant place for flying squirrels and red tree voles (*Arborimus longicaudus*) to live. They like to eat the lichens that only grow on aged trees and can survive for generations without visiting the ground.

WHY LEAVES CHANGE COLOR In the fall (autumn) nature puts on a fantastic show of reds, yellows, oranges, and even purples as the green pigment chlorophyll in the leaves of deciduous trees breaks down, allowing a rainbow of hidden colors to become visible. Chlorophyll makes leaves green and works hard in the tree's food-production department until the fall, when it takes a well-earned winter break until spring. The hidden colored pigments are always present in the leaf, but are overpowered by the dominant green chlorophyll. The yellow and orange colors come from carotenoid pigments and the reds from anthocyanin pigments.

Go on a Leaf Hunt

When exploring the woods, see how many different leaves you can spot. Here are some tips for identifying the leaves you've found:

❋ Touch a leaf and feel its texture—is it glossy, rough, smooth, hairy, or downy?

❋ In season, the flowers and fruits (or nuts, which are fruits in a hard case) will also help you to name the tree.

❋ Have a go at BioBlitzing (see page 7); perhaps you could count the number of tree species in a given area. Blitzing sounds a little destructive—which naturalists aren't. Remember to only leave behind your own footprints.

❋ A pocket tree guide or phone app will help confirm a tree's I.D.

Finding Needles in the Woods

Telling pines, firs, and spruces apart is all about I.D., which takes practice. Here are some helpful needle facts:

❋ Pine trees have bundles of needles in twos to fives. The size may vary, but if a tree has a pack of needles (more than one needle), then it is a pine tree. Spruce and fir needles don't grow in bundles.

❋ Check out the needle—if it has sides, rather than being round or flat, then it's a spruce. A fir needle is flat and won't roll.

Some Common Woodland Trees

As you walk in the woods, look for different plants through the seasons, such as winter snowdrops and spring bluebells, as well as broadleaved trees that shed their leaves in the fall (autumn) and have flowers that develop into fruits. Coniferous trees don't have flowers, but produce seeds inside cones.

THE WILD CHERRY (*Prunus avium*) has flowers that hang in clusters and are an early source of nectar for visiting bees. The birds enjoy eating its fruit—perhaps this is why it's sometimes called the sweet bird cherry. In Scotland it is called the gean. Small mammals (at ground level) enjoy eating fallen wild cherries too.

THE ELDER (*Sambucus nigra*) roots with ease and grows with speed. It fills gaps in hedgerows and, given the chance, bushes into woods too, but it's a spindly tree. Elderflower blossom is honey-scented and a favorite with nectar-gathering honeybees. You can use the blossom to make elderflower syrup. In fall (autumn), the Lilliputian berries are just the right size for a fairy's table or you can use them to make syrups or jams. These berries are rich in Vitamin C, but you may need to add sugar if you cook with them. Use a stick to pull down high branches to pick the blossom and berries.

THE CRAB APPLE (*Malus sylvestris*) is a beautiful tree with spring blossom that attracts bees and lots of other flying insects. Robins, starlings, greenfinches, and thrushes are particularly fond of its tiny apples in the fall (autumn). Don't bite into these apples, though—they are tart and best taken into your wild kitchen. They are packed with pectin, which helps jams and jellies to set. The crab apple tree is common in cities and parkland too.

THE SYCAMORE (*Acer pseudoplatanus*) Sycamores grow in the shade; in fact, they aren't fussy where they grow. In the United Kingdom, where the sycamore is non-native, people who disliked the tree used to hold "syccie bashing" events to remove this invasive tree. Indeed, some conservationists worry that alien species are ecologically harmful. However, non-native species that aren't damaging natural species can sometimes help us out, especially when native species become diseased. The familiar sycamore keys, which are such fun to watch as they flutter and spiral to the ground in the fall (autumn), are formed from a cluster of olive flowers that are pollinated by insects.

Sycamore key

Other Woodland Plants to Spot

Spring is the best time to look for woodland flowers before the ferns and nettles grow too high. See how many of the following you can spot on walks throughout the year.

Wood sorrel (*Oxalis acetosella*) flowers in woods in mid- to late spring. This little white flower is a helpful weathervane, closing its petals at the first hint of any rain. On sunny days it will help you keep track of the time because its petals close as it starts to go dark. The pretty, heart-shaped leaves look like clover but taste of lemon. You can use both wood sorrel and sheep sorrel (*Rumex acetosella*) to give a lemon flavor in cooking.

Snowdrops (*Galanthus* spp.) Galanthophiles are snowdrop lovers and some snowdrop varieties are much sought after. In the United Kingdom, in February 2015 a snowdrop fan paid US$2,120 (£1,390) for a *Galanthus plicatus* bulb. There are hundreds of hybrid snowdrops, most of which grow in gardens and churchyards, but some carpet woods from mid-winter to early spring.

Woodruff (*Galium odoratum*) is another white spring woodland flower. Confusingly, although "odor" appears in its Latin name, it doesn't have a strong scent. However, there is a scented clue in one of its local names: sweet scented bedstraw. This is because dried woodruff (unlike fresh) is scented thanks to a chemical called coumarin. In the past, woodruff was used to scent rooms and linen, just as we use lavender and roses today. Pick woodruff from mid- to late spring, tie it in a bunch, and leave to dry. It will scent a room and keep moths away.

Bluebells (*Hyacinthoides non-scripta*) are native to British woods, but are sadly under threat from the invasive Spanish bluebell (*Hyacinthoides hispanica*). A walk in a native bluebell wood is something any child or adult living in or visiting the United Kingdom should do in spring.

Wild garlic (*Allium ursinum*) You might smell ramsons or wild garlic before you see them. Like bluebells, they carpet damp woodland and moist banks. Use the flowers and leaves to give a garlic flavor in cooking. Pick a leaf, squeeze it in your hand, and you will smell garlic.

Ferns are ancient plants and were once the main vegetation covering Earth. They pre-date the evolution of humans. A scientist who studies ancient plant life is called a paleobotanist. Paleobotanists are interested in living ferns, but also in extinct ferns that dinosaurs munched on. The study of ferns is called pteridology. Like mushrooms, ferns send out spores, rather than seeds (see page 42).

Use a magnifying glass to look closely at fern sori—those that are ragged-looking have probably already released their spores.

Under a delicate fern frond are spore cases called sporangia that are filled with hundreds of dust-like spores. You can see these scale-like bumps on the underside of the fronds. A cluster of sporangia is called a sorus. Sori are ripe and ready to release their spores when they turn brown (in mid-summer).

Horsetails (*Equisetum* spp.) reproduce using spores rather than seeds—like their close relatives, the ferns. The first stems appear in spring and are topped with brown, cone-like structures that bear the spores. Later in the year, you'll see larger stems with tough, stringy leaves that give the plant its feathery, horsetail appearance. Horsetails spread quickly—in fact, they are considered invasive in some areas. Horsetails are living fossils, being the only surviving members of the class Equisetopsida. For more than a 100 million years, Equisetopsida plants, stretching up to 98ft (30m) high, dominated forest floors of the late Mesozoic period (254–65 million years ago).

Bilberries (*Vaccinium myrtillus*) are tiny, but delicious. These plants grow on moors and in mature woods—look for the greenish-pink flowers in spring and pick the dark blue fruit in late summer. Bilberries may be called huckleberries or whortleberries but, whatever the name, they're not blueberries. They are, however, just the right size for grazing on. You'll have to be quick, though, because insects, birds, rodents, and deer like them too. The juice stains fingers and you may find yourself with a bilberry moustache. Not surprisingly, the berries were once used as a dye (see *Inks and Dyes*, on pages 64–65).

Wild Garlic Pesto

This recipe makes one small bowl of pesto. Lightly toast ¼ cup (25g) pine nuts, either in the oven or a dry skillet (frying pan) over a low heat (see *Seaside Sprinkles*, on page 155). Be very careful if you're using an oven because the pine nuts will suddenly go brown—it's easy to burn them. Next place three big handfuls of wild garlic and 1oz (25g) Parmesan cheese, along with the toasted pine nuts, in a food-processor and blitz briefly to blend all the ingredients. Add about ½ cup (100ml) extra virgin olive oil (or enough oil to make a thick paste) and some freshly ground black pepper if you wish. Place the yummy green pesto in a small bowl, cover, and keep in a refrigerator for up to 10 days. You can use young nettle or dandelion leaves instead of the wild garlic, but you'll need to add a clove of garlic. You can also mix finely chopped wild garlic leaves with butter to make garlic butter.

Woodland Broom

This type of broom is called a besom. Traditionally, the handle is made from hazel (*Corylus* spp.) branches and the head from birch (*Betula* spp.) twigs, but you can use whatever you find when exploring the woods. Just check that the broom will fit the witch or wizard it's being made for. Try to find a smooth handle that doesn't have any knobbles.

WHAT TO USE

- ✔ Penknife and/or potato peeler
- ✔ A long stick (about the thickness of a broom handle)
- ✔ Garden plant wire
- ✔ Lots of thin twigs, about 14in (35cm) in length and ½in (1cm) in diameter
- ✔ Strong string

WHAT TO DO

1. Use the penknife or potato peeler to smooth away any knobbles or tiny branches on the stick (the broom handle). If you wish, you can carefully strip away the bark to make the stick smooth, or leave the bark on so that your broom has character.

2. Lay the stick on the ground and slip a length of plant wire under the bottom at the point where you want to tie the twigs to the broom to make the brush.

3. Weave the wire around each of the twigs as you attach them to the broom handle. When you have enough twigs in place on the first side, wind the wire around the handle to secure the twigs.

4   Turn the broom over and repeat the process on the other side. You can add more layers of twigs to each side to make a thicker brush if you wish.

5   When you have completed the layers, wind some string very tightly around the finished brush. It's a good idea to wind the string round lots of times to produce a cordage collar. This will look neat and also secure the twigs firmly to the handle. Tie the string as tightly as you can.

6   You are now ready to sweep the leaves from your wigwam or den floor.

Broom Construction Tip

If you are making the broom at home, rather than in the woods, you can achieve a neater and stronger finish by sticking some carpet tape on top of the string around the broom handle. Then wrap a strip of burlap (hessian) sacking over the tape—ensuring it's wide enough to hide the tape and long enough to wrap twice around the twigs—and tie it in a bow.

Trunks and Branches

The different parts of a tree enable it to function as an entire system. Trees are big plants, but you can look in detail at each of the parts. Feel the bark's texture and examine it with a magnifying glass. Collect leaves and seeds, and study the tree's roots. A woodland's history is in the trees themselves. After dark, a woodland is full of unexpected noises—plan a night visit with family and friends to see what wildlife passes by.

TRUNKS AND BARK

Tree bark has different colors and patterns. It may be spotty, look like a messed-up jigsaw, or have dashes or stripes. Looking at the bark will help you I.D. the tree. Carving the name or initials of somebody you love on a tree is something that's been done for centuries. A sad, broken-hearted lover may have carved his beloved's initials on a tree. Or perhaps the carving was made by a happy lover who walked in the woods with his or her partner. A carved message on a tree is a very public love letter that doesn't need a stamp. The Ancient Roman poet Virgil wrote in Eclogue X: *"Well, I know that in the woods, amid wild beasts' dens, it is better to suffer and carve my love on the young trees. They will grow, and you, my love, will grow with them."*

In Northern Nevada, the Basque sheepherders who sought their fortunes in the American West carved on aspen trees (*Populus tremuloides*). These historical carvings, which are called arborglyphs, provide an interesting record of the experiences and thoughts of the sheepherders. An expert carver knew which trees to pick and how to engrave a lasting message. They would be shocked to know that arborglyph scholars are now keen to read these private messages. The aspen is one of the hundred most common trees in North America. It grows quickly and colonizes disturbed areas (from fire and landslides etc.), but the aspen's lifespan is short because of fungal diseases. Today, it is illegal to carve on trees in national parks and grasslands.

A tree's life depends on the surrounding climate—including the temperature and levels of water and sunlight—as well as soil conditions, storms, and, sadly, forest fires. *Any tree that doesn't adapt to its surroundings will not survive.* The bark of a mature tree is much rougher than that of a younger tree, and its trunk is usually larger. Some trees, such as the silver birch (*Betula pendula*), grow quickly. This is a grown-up tree by the age of 40. In contrast, an oak tree (*Quercus* spp.) takes hundreds of years to reach maturity. The oldest Douglas fir (*Pseudotsuga menziesii*) in the United Kingdom was raised from a seed brought back from its native North America in 1826. This tree is in the grounds of Scone Palace, in Perthshire, Scotland. The world's tallest conifer that isn't a redwood is a Douglas fir in Coos County, Oregon, at almost 328ft (100m). If a tree grows taller than this, the pull of gravity makes it difficult for water to be transported throughout the tree.

TELL THE AGE OF A TREE When a tree has died or been cut down, you can look at the growth rings in an open section of trunk and age the tree. Each band is made up of two rings: a lighter ring (the spring growth) and a darker band (the late-summer growth). The older rings are closest to the center of the tree. The ring sizes

Tree rings

may differ but this doesn't matter; it still counts as a year of the tree's life. A wide ring means the tree grew well that year and a narrower ring that its growth was stunted. For example, the rings will be thicker in wet and warmer years, but narrower in years when rainfall is low. A tree's growth can also be affected by snow, levels of sunlight, and temperature, as well as how crowded it is by other trees. Studying the rings (ideally, with a magnifying glass) will tell you a lot about a tree's growth. The wind can also shape trees—you can see this on windswept hills, where a prevailing wind has dried out the new growth buds on one side. Dendrochronology is the study of change through tree ring growth. You can also estimate the age of a pine tree by counting the whorls where the branches have grown out.

GO TREE HUGGING

Find a tree you can reach all the way round with your arms and give it a hug. Or, perhaps find a bigger tree and link arms with friends to hug the tree.

Hug a tree

PLAY TREE TAG

Have a fun game of tag in the woods and choose a special tree to be home. Run from the chaser, touch the tree, and you are safe.

GO TREE BARK RUBBING

You can make your own bark rubbings and write personal messages on these if you wish. Future generations will be able to read your thoughts if you stick the labeled rubbings in a scrapbook. You will need some sheets of white paper, wax crayons, and sticky tape. Simply hold a piece of white paper against a tree (or tape the paper to the trunk) as you color with a wax crayon. The ridges and bumps of the bark will appear on your paper. Crayon gently, especially over big knobbles in the bark. Collect rubbings from different tree species. Name the tree, date the rubbings, and then mount them in a scrapbook or keep them in a poly-pocket file.

Bark rubbing

TWIGS AND STICKS

The counting nursery rhyme suggests picking up sticks at numbers five and six: "*One, two, buckle my shoe. Three, four, knock at the door. Five, six, pick up sticks.*" But what can you do with them when you've picked them up? Here are a few suggestions for having fun with twigs and sticks outdoors:

✳ Wild walkers find a stick shaped like a shepherd's staff helpful.

✳ Wild artists draw in mud or on sand with short sturdy sticks.

✳ Wild cooks use sticks to toast marshmallows or bannocks (a type of bread) by a campfire. Younger children may need some adult help to do this.

✳ Sticks make instant magic wands for wild wizards and fairies.

✳ Use a twig to stir magic portions or wild scents.

✳ Skilful wild warriors bend sticks to make bows and carve points to make arrows.

✳ Wild soldiers use sticks bound together in battle.

✳ Some stick thoughts:
  - What is the difference between a twig and a stick?

  - Some dictionaries say that a twig is a branch without leaves, but is a branch a stick?

  - Does a stick need to be made out of wood?

  - Does size make a difference?

  - Think about the sticks you play games with. What wood is your cricket bat, or lacrosse or hockey stick made from?

MAKE A SIMPLE DREAM CATCHER Native Americans made dream catchers to protect them from bad dreams while they slept. Good dreams would pass through the hole in the center of the dream catcher and slip down the feathers to the person sleeping below. The feather meant life or a breath of air. The type of feather used was important. An owl's feather was for wisdom and an eagle's for courage. The Native Americans would have woven natural thread (see *Make Nettle Cordage*, on page 54) across the circle to catch the bad dreams. The bad dreams were trapped in the web and disappeared at dawn. To make a dream catcher, simply hoop a bendy stick—perhaps from a willow tree (*Salix* spp.)—to make a circle. Secure the circle with cordage or string. Create the web by tying a knot in the thread at the top of the hoop and then winding the thread around and inside the hoop to create a spider's web. Hang a feather from the completed dream catcher.

Bad dreams are trapped in the web and disappear at dawn

Make a Woodland Star

The idea for this star evolved from the dream catchers used by Native Americans. This star is for decorative purposes only, but you can easily adapt it to become a dream catcher if you wish.

WHAT TO USE

- ✔ 6 dry sticks, about 12in (30cm) in length
- ✔ String
- ✔ Scissors
- ✔ Double-sided sticky tape
- ✔ Wild treasures

WHAT TO DO

1. Lay three sticks on the ground in the shape of a triangle, with the ends overlapping, and use small lengths of string to tie them together.

2. Repeat to make a second triangle with the remaining sticks. Place one triangle on top of the other so that it looks like a star.

3. Tie the two triangles tightly together with some more string to make the star.

4. Tie a length of string at the top of the star so that you can hang it from a tree.

5. Hang two or three lengths of sticky tape from the bottom of the star.

6. Use your imagination to decorate the star by attaching wild treasures, such as leaves, twigs, and seeds, to the frame and also sticking some "wildness" to the sticky tape. Don't use anything too heavy (e.g. a very big fir cone).

Build a Woodland Wigwam

Create a private den near your favorite tree and have fun creating a little home of your own in the woods. You can use your den as a hideout while you watch and study woodland wildlife.

WHAT TO BRING

✔ Rope and/or string
✔ Scissors or a penknife

WHAT TO FIND

✔ A tree in a glade
✔ Fallen branches (e.g. from beech and birch trees)
✔ Logs and/or large stones
✔ Twigs
✔ Ferns
✔ Moss, heather, or dried leaves (depending on the season)

WHAT TO DO

1. Find a tree standing alone in a glade. Other trees are fine, but a stand-alone tree will give you more space to work in.

2. Search for large branches to lean against the trunk of the tree. It is better to use several thinner branches, if possible, than a smaller number of bigger branches as they will be easier to maneuver. Also look out for logs or stones to put at the base of the branches to hold them in place.

3. Use rope or string to tie the branches individually to the tree. You can also tie the branches to each other, but the wigwam will be more stable—and less likely to collapse—if each branch is tied individually. You can use the spider's web of string created when tying on the branches to support the ferns later on.

4. Now that you have the basic structure, start weaving twigs between the branches, particularly at the base. You can use some string to help you here too.

5. Begin to fill in all of the gaps with dense layers of fern.

6. Use moss, heather, ferns, or leaves to cover the floor of the wigwam and place logs inside to sit on.

Make a Miniature Den and Garden

You could also build a miniature den and garden, perhaps for a stick person to live in (see *Fun Flower and Stick People*, on page 52). Build the den using twigs and, for ease, use a tree trunk as a back-supporting wall. Use twigs, bark, leaves, nuts, hips, haws, cones, mosses, ferns, lichen, burs, conker cases, and horsetails to create little homes and gardens. Just look around for inspiration for your house-building and wild garden landscaping. Here are some ideas for using the things you find:

❋ Lay twigs on the ground to make decking and paths. Use fir cones as trees or hedging and weave cleavers, honeysuckle, acorns, conkers, and burs into fences.

❋ Use some grass or moss to make an instant lawn.

❋ Use horsetails and fern leaflets (from a frond) as mini trees and cut common wild flowers and bright berries to create some pretty flowerbeds.

Make a Catapult

You can have lots of fun in the woods with a catapult. Hazel trees provide the strongest wood for catapults, so look for these when you're hunting for a Y-shaped piece of wood. Crab apple (*Malus sylvestris*) wood is also a good choice. Remember never to fire your catapult at any living thing. This is an adaptation of the author Abi Elphinstone's guide to making a catapult.

WHAT TO BRING

✔ Penknife and/or potato peeler
✔ Garden cutters (optional)
✔ 2 large rubber bands

WHAT TO FIND

✔ Y-shaped piece of wood
✔ Fir cones (for firing)

WHAT TO DO

1. Find a Y-shaped piece of wood when you're next in the woods. You may be lucky and find one on the ground; otherwise, ask an adult to help you use the penknife or garden cutters to chop a branch from a tree.

2. Use the penknife to cut the piece of wood down to the size you want—8in (20cm) is a good length to aim for if you're measuring from the tip of one of the Y-prongs to the end of the handle. Make sure the length of wood beneath the Y-prongs (the handle) is long enough for you to clasp your full palm around.

3. This step is optional, but fun. Carefully use the penknife (or potato peeler) to whittle away the bark from the wood. You could leave the bark on the handle and carve your initials into it.

4. Use the penknife or potato peeler to make a groove, 1in (2.5cm) from the tip, around each of the Y-prongs.

5. Position the two rubber bands in the grooves in the Y-frame. Use one hand to hold a fir cone firmly inside the other ends of the rubber bands, pull back, and fire.

Strengthen your catapult
When you get home, you can strengthen your catapult by placing it in a warm oven for 10 minutes. If you wish, you could also coat the catapult with craft varnish once it has cooled—this will make it stronger.

Look very carefully for the best stick to make your catapult.

Leaves, Flowers, and Fruits

Young naturalists can study the leaves of different trees, as well as their flowers and fruit. As the leaves fall to the ground, look at them closely and enjoy their striking colors.

FUN IN THE FALL

Fall (autumn) is one of the most exciting times to go on a woodland walk, especially if you're in a wood where deciduous trees outnumber evergreens (trees that carry leaves all year round). Plan to visit just before the leaves fall to the ground. The bright reds and golden yellows in nature's leafy paintbox are so colorful—you may forget that the falling leaves signal the end of summer. In the fall, the maples (*Acer* spp.) of North West America, in particular, are breathtaking. Red maples turn crimson, black maples turn gold, while sugar maples can be fiery red, yellow, or orange. Sometimes the beautiful colors can be enjoyed in the heat of an Indian summer. The autumn equinox is when the sun is directly over the equator and the length of day and night is equal, but then daylight hours start to shorten. Lack of sunlight and cooler air temperatures trigger the changing color of the leaves on a deciduous tree as it prepares for winter. A deciduous tree puts life on hold, just as some wildlife hibernates.

What is Photosynthesis?

Leaves need sunlight (energy) to convert carbon dioxide from the atmosphere and water from the soil into sugar (food) and oxygen in a process called photosynthesis. Leaves are a tree's food factory. The leaves take in carbon dioxide and release oxygen through tiny holes called stomata. Here is an equation for photosynthesis:

LIGHT

v

CARBON DIOXIDE + WATER > SUGAR + OXYGEN

A tree's food pipes are blocked off as the days shorten in the fall (autumn), allowing it to conserve water in winter. After a leaf is sealed off from the stem, it will drift to the ground.

Have Fun with Leaves

As well as crunching through fallen leaves, there is lots of leafy fun to be had in the woods. Have a go at the following:

✳ Stop, look, and listen as the leaves fall to the ground (see *The Sound of Wild Silence*, on page 13).

✳ Find an area of clear ground and draw a picture using some twigs and fallen leaves.

✳ Pile up some dry leaves to make a comfy chair to sink into while you check out leaf I.D.s in your pocket guide or on your phone.

✳ Have a leaf fight, but be aware that hedgehogs, which are in decline, enjoy living in leaves.

✳ Stick different types of leaf on both sides of some double-sided sticky tape and then I.D. the trees that the leaves have come from. You could hang the leaf strips over a branch or loop and fasten a small strip to create a woodland head-dress. Stick small pieces of fern or fir between the colorful leaves to add some greenery if you wish.

Stick some leaves to double-sided tape or create tree-trunk art.

HORSE CHESTNUT TREES AND CONKERS

If you touch the buds of a horse chestnut tree (*Aesculus hippocastanum*) in winter, they feel sticky with resin, which protects the new leaves from frost. When the sun melts the resin, horse chestnut leaves are among the first to unfurl in spring. Later, when the tree comes into flower, it looks magnificent as its white, candelabra-like blossoms dance in the breeze. Look in the center of the flower and see what color it is. Research suggests that red-centered flowers have been pollinated, while yellow-centered flowers will still attract insects to be pollinated. The leaves from previous seasons leave horseshoe-shaped scars on the twigs. The buds of the red-flowered horse chestnut (*Aesculus* x *carnea*), which is a hybrid (a cross between two different species), aren't as sticky.

Horse chestnut trees cast useful shade on a hot summer's day. We must, however, wait until fall (autumn) for conkers to arrive. These fruits, which ripen in early to mid-fall, are protected by prickly green cases. Inside sit mahogany conkers, which give their name to the famous game. It is quite tricky removing the conkers from the cases, but there is usually more than one conker inside. The cases of the red chestnut are smoother and easier to break into. Unlike the sweet chestnuts that are often roasted at Christmas, horse chestnuts should not be eaten because they can be toxic.

OHIO—THE BUCKEYE STATE The buckeye tree (*Aesculus glabra*) is from the same family as the horse chestnut and is Ohio's state tree. Native Americans in Ohio used to call the fruit hetuck, or "eye of the buck."

Some Conker Crafts

Conkers can be used to make jewelry and to craft small animals or doll house furniture. Here are some creative ideas for you to try:

MAKE A CONKER NECKLACE Thread some conkers onto a piece of string to make a necklace or garland (see Make Flower Jewelry, on page 56).

MAKE A HEDGEHOG Stick some shortened toothpicks (cocktail sticks) into the back of a conker to make a hedgehog. A conker in the corner of a room is said to keep spiders away. This is because it contains a natural, soap-like chemical compound called saponin. Perhaps you could try out this spider theory with your conker hedgehog. Others say that if a conker is split, it will keep moths at bay.

MAKE CONKER FURNITURE To make a stool or table, carefully push four pins (with colored heads if possible) into the non-shiny side of a conker to make the legs. If necessary, make small holes with a skewer or small precision screwdriver first.

To make a chair, push four colored pins into the underside of a conker (as for a stool). Push four or five more pins an equal distance apart, along one of the long upper sides of the conker. Weave 2¼in (6cm) strands of colored yarn in and out of the pin slats to make the chair back. Wind and knot each strand of yarn around the pins at the start and end of the chair back. (You may find it easier to pin the "chair back" pins into a pincushion while you weave and then transfer the back of the chair to the conker when it is finished.)

Play a Game of Conkers

The name "conker" may come from the word *conqueror* or originate from the word *conche* because the game was originally played with conch shells (snail shells). The first recorded game of conkers took place on the Isle of Wight, in England, in 1848. You need two players for a game of conkers.

WHAT TO USE

✔ Firm, unblemished conker
✔ Vinegar or salt
✔ Small bowl
✔ Clear nail polish (optional)
✔ Skewer
✔ Piece of string, 10in (25cm) in length

WHAT TO DO

If you're playing this game in the wild, you don't need to prepare the conkers first. However, everyone wants a winning conker, so try strengthening the conker by soaking it in a bowl of vinegar or salt water overnight or painting it with clear nail polish. (You can also store conkers in a dark cupboard for a year.) Whatever you decide, the first step is to hunt for firm, unblemished conkers. Skewer a hole through the center of the conker. When you've made a hole all the way through, thread the conker onto the piece of string and tie a knot at the end. You're now ready to play conkers.

THE CONKER GAME RULES ARE:

1. Traditionally, the first player is the person who is the first to say: "*Obli, obli, O, My first go.*"

2. Player One then holds the conker dangling from its string as still as possible.

3. Player Two—the striker—wraps his or her conker string around one hand and holds the conker in the other hand. He or she then releases the conker to strike Player One's conker. If Player Two misses, up to two further goes are allowed.

4. On striking the player traditionally says: "*Obli, obli, onker. My nut will conker.*"

5. If the strings get tangled, then the first player to shout "strings" gets an extra shot. If a player drops the conker, the other player can shout "stamps," and stamp on the conker. If, however, the owner shouts "stamps" first, then stamps is disallowed and the conker bashing continues.

6. Once Player Two has made a strike, Player One then takes turn as striker. The game continues until one of the conkers is so badly bashed that it can't be used. The conker that hasn't been destroyed is the winner.

Conker Fame

A conker gains fame as it destroys opponents' conkers—two bashed conkers and the winning conker is a two-er. If a conker has beaten ten other conkers, then it is a ten-er. Good luck in getting a fifty-er. Remember that a two-er can beat a ten-er and some rules allow you to add the number of "ers" that your victim has gained e.g. if the conker that you destroyed was a three-er, you can add three to your conker's "ers"). Look after your conkers because there can be fewer conkers (and hazelnuts etc.) in some years than others.

Leaf Bunting

This bunting project takes a while to complete, but you can break the instructions down into easy stages and do a little bit at a time. Leaves with the same shape have been used here, but you can vary the species and colors if you wish. The finished bunting makes a natural decoration.

WHAT TO USE

- ✔ Isosceles triangle or flag-shaped cardboard template, with two sides measuring 5–6in (12–15cm)
- ✔ Enough newspaper for 15 pieces of bunting
- ✔ Iron and ironing board
- ✔ 3–4 pieces of wax (greaseproof) paper, measuring 8 x 8in (20 x 20cm), depending on the leaf size
- ✔ 15 pressed leaves (see *Press Wild Flowers and Grasses*, on page 55)
- ✔ Grater
- ✔ Wax crayons
- ✔ Glue
- ✔ Long piece of string or nettle cordage (see *Make Nettle Cordage*, on page 54), for hanging the bunting
- ✔ Stapler

WHAT TO DO

1 Use the cardboard template to cut a triangular shape from the bottom of the pieces of newspaper. You can create any shape you want, but make sure the top edge that you will attach to the cordage or string is straight.

2 Cover the center of the ironing board with some newspaper. Place one of the squares of wax (greaseproof) paper on top of the newspaper and put a pressed leaf in one half of the square.

3 Grate a few pieces of wax crayon over the leaf. Do not grate too much.

4 Fold the other half of the wax (greaseproof) paper over the leaf to cover it. Press a hot iron over the paper to melt the crayon—this should take no more than 5–6 seconds. The wax will stick to the leaf.

5. Repeat with a variety of colored crayons until all of the leaves have been colored. Replace the piece of wax (greaseproof) paper as necessary.

6. Glue a leaf (with the colored side facing outward) to the center of a piece of newspaper bunting. Leave enough paper at the top to make a 1in (2.5cm) fold for attaching the bunting to the string or cordage. Repeat until you have used all the leaves.

7. Fold the top of the first piece of bunting over the string or cordage and secure neatly at each end with the stapler. Leave enough space for sliding the bunting along the string or cordage.

8. Attach the rest of the pieces of bunting in the same way, making sure you space them out evenly. Display your length of bunting outside or indoors.

Variation

BUNTING LEAF PRINTS

You might like to make some bunting using leaf prints instead. Find as many differently shaped and sized leaves as you can and use newspaper or white or colored paper for the bunting. Protect your work surface with newspaper and have your paints ready. Paint the upper side of each leaf and then press this down firmly onto the bunting. Remove the leaf to reveal the leaf's print.

Fascinating Fungi

Foraging chanterelles

There are millions of fungi species, so even mycologists (people who study fungi) have much to learn. If you've touched fungi, it's important to wash your hands before eating. Some people like to wear gloves, but this means you can't feel a fungus' texture.

WHAT ARE FUNGI?

The mushrooms and toadstools that you see above ground are the "fruiting bodies" of fungi. These are simple, non-green organisms and are not part of the plant kingdom. Fungi are, in fact, in a group of their own. Hidden underground is the more permanent mycelium, which is made up of branching, thread-like cells. It is important not to disturb this underground network, which is a complex series of food tubes. Fairies are said to play in the fairy rings you sometimes see in the woods, but these are made naturally by some fungi as a result of a particular pattern of mycelium growth.

The fruit (the mushroom or toadstool) appears above ground when the fungus is ready to produce new spores (these are produced by non-flowering plants to reproduce). This structure's sole purpose is to produce spores. Spores are dispersed by wind, rain, and insects, just as plant seeds are (see *Seed Dispersal*, on page 60). If you kick a toadstool, you can help spread the spores. Next step is the growth of the mycelium and then a tiny mushroom pops through something called a universal veil, which covers the growing mushroom, and the cycle starts all over again.

Mushrooms are mysterious and some look very weird. Fungi go hand-in-glove with falling leaves. You can find mushrooms in the hills and along waysides, but you'll find a wider variety in forests and woodlands. Fungi provide

Chanterelle mushrooms

food and shelter for many insects and help trees and plants grow by recycling nutrients in the soil. They feed on living organisms: plants, animals, and decaying organic matter. No chlorophyll is involved—fungi survive in darkness.

IDENTIFYING FUNGI You can use the size, color, shape, smell, texture, and location to identify fungi. But correct I.D. is from the fungus' spores. Both poisonous and edible fungi form fairy rings. Some good fungus I.D. questions to ask yourself include:

✻ Where is the fungus growing? Is it in woodland or grassland, on manure or wood, or near a particular plant? Lots of mushrooms are associated with certain tree species. Yellow, apricot-scented chanterelle mushrooms (*Cantharellus cibarius*), for example, often grow near beech trees (*Fagus* spp.). Indeed, many trees need fungi to survive: the fungus gives the

Fungi Can Be Useful... and Dangerous

The antibiotic penicillin (discovered in 1928 by Alexander Fleming) comes from a fungus (as do medicines called statins which help lower cholesterol). So, medicine needs fungi. Fungi are also vital in fermentation, a chemical reaction that's used in the production of lots of foods and drinks, including bread, cheese, wine, and beer. However, some fungi cause disease in plants and animals, and poison humans. Remember: always wash your hands after touching fungi and don't suck your fingers or chew your fingernails when handling them.

Chicken of the woods

tree water and minerals, while the tree feeds the fungus in a relationship of joint benefit that is known as a mycorrhiza (see *The Fungal Internet*, on page 18).

❋ Bracket fungi like King Alfred's cakes (*Daldinia concentrica*) grow directly on the tree. Also look out for the bright orange chicken of the woods (*Laetiporus sulphureus*), which grows throughout summer on standing or fallen trees, especially oaks, wild cherries, and willows. The fibers of this mushroom look like chicken flesh. Beefsteak fungus (*Fistulina hepatica*), which looks like liver, is another meaty fungus.

❋ Is the fungus shaped like a trumpet? If so, it may be a chanterelle or a horn of plenty (*Craterellus cornucopioides*).

❋ Is the fungus smelly, sticky, smooth, or scaly?

❋ Does the mushroom have gills? If so, are they crowded or well spaced? Field mushrooms (*Agaricus campestris*) and fly agarics have gills.

STUDYING FUNGUS SPORES Collect a mature fungus from the woods and carefully remove any stalk from the mushroom cap. Place the cap on a piece of black card with the gill or spongy side facing down. Cover the cap with a small bowl to stop it drying out. Remove the bowl and cap 24 hours later—you should see a print of the spores. Mushrooms may release white, black, rust-brown, or even pink spores. Black spore prints are easier to see on white paper. Spray the spore print with hairspray and leave to dry. Don't leave the mushroom covered for more than 24 hours or you may encourage fungi larvae to emerge. Try using different colored cards and building up a library of spore prints. Label, date, and note the place where each mushroom was picked. If you have ever noticed colored dust covering a leaf or the ground beneath a mushroom, you've probably witnessed a spore print in its natural setting.

Some Interesting Fungi

The top three lookers on my fungi catwalk are golden spindles (*Clavulinopsis fusiformis*), which looks like thin, golden fingers; an ear-shaped fungus called Jew or jelly ear (*Auricularia auricula-judae*); and orange peel (*Aleuria aurantia*), which is as pretty as any flower. Like some other fungi, orange peel fires tiny drops of fluid (called Buller's drops) vertically, often as many as a million times a day: load and fire, repeat, load and fire, time and time again. This discovery was made by author and naturalist Beatrix Potter (see page 9) and her mycologist friend Arthur Buller. The following is a shortlist of fungi to look for:

Giant puffball (*Calvatia gigantea*) This doesn't have gills, but you will disperse thousands of spores if you kick a puffball.

Puffball

Cauliflower fungus (*Sparassis crispa*) This edible, but funny-looking, mushroom is named after the vegetable, but looks like a brain.

Witches' butter (*Dacrymyces palmatus*) This is a yellow fungus that grows on moss-covered logs—it looks like a blob of melting butter. Vomit slime (*Fuligo septica*) is another slime-like fungi that's slimy by name too.

Fly agaric or fly amanita (*Amanita muscaria*) This poisonous mushroom likes growing near birch trees. With its familiar red cap and white spots, it would make a fine centerpiece for a fairy conference in the woods.

Bleeding broadleaf crust (*Stereum rugosum*) This is a crust or bracket fungus that grows on trees. If you mark an X on the fungus with your fingernail, it will bleed blood red. This is because the tissue has been exposed to air. Look at it under a lens and touch it—it will feel rough.

Scarlet elf mushroom (*Sarcoscypha coccinea*) Most fungi grow in the fall (autumn), but this spring mushroom is perfect for a fairy garden. It is bright and goblet-shaped—just right for elves to drink from. Although red, which may make you think of danger, it isn't poisonous. Your elves could use yellow fairy cups or lemon discos (*Bisporella citrina*) to drink from too.

Scarlet elf

Hat thrower (*Pilobolus* spp.) You may think a cheetah is the fastest animal on Earth, but, allowing for scale, the dung-loving hat thrower fungus is the winner. It looks like a tiny translucent snake in a bowler hat (which contains the spores). This fungus throws its hat fast. It is eaten by grass-eating herbivores (such as cows), digested, and then pooped out. This is how the hat thrower begins life—growing on top of dung. To start the cycle again, the hat thrower needs to get out of the poop zone and reach fresh grass. So, the spore is fired rapidly out of the dung, accelerating faster than all guns.

Be a Woodland Detective

There are lots of things to look out for during a walk in the woods. Look closely and you'll be able to see which birds and animals inhabit the area. You may not be lucky enough to see some of the animals themselves, but you should be able to spot and study the clues they leave behind. (To learn more about finding wild animals, see *Tracking Wildlife*, on pages 122–23.)

LOOK AND LEARN TASK 1: BARK AND HOLES

Look at tree trunk damage. It may have been nibbled by wildlife such as deer or rabbits that can't climb a tree, but what about mice—some of them can scamper up trees. Here are some more clues to help woodland detectives work out which creatures are in the woods:

✻ Upper trunk damage may be the work of a woodpecker or squirrel.

✻ Look for loose bark, where bats may roost.

✻ Look for a woodpecker's hole.

✻ Is the tree being used as a no-build roof for a burrowing animal? Perhaps for a fox, badger, rabbit, mouse, or vole?

✻ Look for heaps of cones—squirrels pile up cones to mark out their territory.

✻ Check out the size of the tunnel and compare this with the body widths of different animals.

✻ Look for mosses and lichens (abundant lichen growth is a sign of good air quality).

✻ Peeling bark may be the result of pollution or the bark's pores being blocked.

Like other rodents, squirrels have four front teeth that never stop growing. This is so that they don't wear down from their constant gnawing.

Listen—is that a woodpecker drilling? How many holes are there? Why did the woodpecker start pecking out another hole close by?

LOOK AND LEARN TASK 2:
WHO ATE THE NUTS, FUNGI, AND CONES?

If you're walking in a wood, look for nuts, fungi, and cones that have been nibbled by wildlife. With practice you'll be able to look at nibbled nuts, fungi, and cones, and work out which creatures have been feasting.

Nuts

✳ A nut that has been coarsely cut in half is the work of a squirrel. Squirrels weigh nuts before opening them—they're smart. They don't waste their efforts on rotten or empty shells. Scientists have, however, played a trick on squirrels by filling two halves of a previously opened hazelnut with sand and then gluing them back together. They found that the squirrels weighed the sand-filled nuts before opening them. Rather a mean experiment, but you could try this out yourself if you find a stash of broken hazelnut shells and know where squirrels are in residence.

✳ A dormouse holds a nut between its paws and turns it, as it chisels a rounded hole that is big enough to remove the kernel from the shell. It's a beautiful piece of craftsmanship that leaves a smooth, round rim. The hole is perfectly finished—a dormouse could be employed as a fairy clog-maker.

Fungi

✳ Slugs make slimy dents.

✳ Birds leave pecked holes.

✳ Look for the incisor tooth marks left by deer.

✳ Mice leave small, gnawed marks.

Cones

✳ Red and gray squirrels leave cones in open spaces with the scales eaten, leaving a clean-cut core.

✳ Mice are neat and tidy nibblers, and the cone will probably be hidden (i.e. not easy to find).

✳ Birds (e.g. woodpeckers) leave cones with ragged edges that are often jammed into holes in the bark of trees. There may be a pile of finished cones on the ground, beneath the cone that you've found in the bark.

Spy on Woodland Bugs

The woods are full of insects to find and examine, so have a go at these bug-hunting activities:

✳ Turn over a small log and study the bugs that are living there. Be very quick and have your magnifying glass at the ready, because the bugs will scurry away from daylight.

✳ Hold a piece of white paper under a hanging branch and gently shake it. Look at the paper and see if any bugs have landed. Carefully put the paper on the ground and investigate further with your magnifying glass.

The Sleepy Dormouse

Common dormice (*Muscardinus avellanarius*) are nocturnal and live in the canopy of deciduous trees, so they are tricky to see. They are the size of a Victoria plum, ginger in color, and have a bushy tail. Dormice use their whiskers to feel their way around or navigate trees. The word dormouse comes from the French verb *dormir* (which means "to sleep"), because dormice sleep a lot—they fall asleep in poor weather and also hibernate from late fall (autumn) to mid-spring when there aren't many insects to eat. In late summer and early fall, they stuff themselves with food and become rotund.

Scientists used to think that dormice preferred to live in hazel coppices, but they also like sycamore trees, because this tree species encourages aphids that the dormice guzzle up—this is an example of a non-native species, the sycamore, helping out an endangered species, the dormouse. Dormice are endangered because they don't produce large families and their ground survival strategy isn't very good since they live in trees. If there is a loss of dormice habitat, then it is difficult for them to reproduce quickly.

SPOT A MEMBER OF THE CERVIDAE FAMILY

This ruminating (grass-eating) family include reindeer, elk, and moose, as well as deer and other species. Deer are herbivores, but also nibble at bark on trees and, although they can't climb trees, they can jump very high. They can also swim and they like eating berries too. I know this because I've seen them swim out to a small isle where bilberries grow. The deer eat the berries and so there is none left for wild food gatherers. All male deer, except for the Chinese water deer (*Hydropotes inermis*), grow new antlers each year. When the antlers are fully grown, they fall off (although a stag may rub at a tree to help remove them). On a winter's walk, the discovery of an antler is the most brilliant nature trophy. It is too big to keep in a nature treasure box, but you could hang it on a wall. The more time you spend in the wild, the greater number of wild treasures you will find.

Bat

Dormouse

Lichen

Vole

Stag

Some Woodland Animals and Plants

Forests and woodlands are home to a wealth of wildlife, providing many species of birds and mammals with food and shelter. In these rich and diverse habitats, you will also find wild flowers such as snowdrops in winter and bluebells in late spring, as well as a host of different mushrooms and toadstool in the fall (autumn).

Woodpecker

Horse chestnuts

Fox

Woodruff

Wild garlic

Rabbit

② Meadows, Hedgerows, and Hills

Summer is when meadow flowers are tall and beautiful. As the weeks pass, so different wild flowers come into bloom. Nature is in control of each passing meadowland scene. Do a handstand in a meadow and see if your legs peep up above the sorrel and buttercups. Lie down among the flowers and listen to the birds and bees, or watch the clouds pass by. After a picnic lunch, fill your forager's trug with hedgerow flowers and fruits. Grab a sturdy stick to help you reach berries, but try not to trample plants as you gather. Fruits are created for plants to reproduce, so don't be greedy. Keep your baskets small and leave some for the birds.

Flowers and Grasses

Grasses vary from short lawn grasses to adult-waist-high reeds and bamboo plants (which can be over 160ft/50m tall). Grasses provide food for animals and some cultivars such as wheat, barley, and oats provide food for humans. Grasses, sedges, and rushes are wind-pollinated flowering plants. They produce far more pollen than brightly colored, or scented, insect-pollinated flowering plants.

FIND THE FLOWERS...

Flowers are often categorized by color in plant guidebooks, but they can also be arranged according to the seasons. The increasingly rare white snowdrop (*Galanthus* spp.) flowers in winter when the land is often crisp and white. Compare this tiny flower, poking though the snow, with a brightly colored bunch of wild flowers picked from a hedgerow in summer.

The types of wild flowers you spot will depend on the habitat in which they grow, as well as the time of year. Up in the hills you will find fewer flowers and trees because the plants growing there have to deal with strong winds and poor soil cover. The flowering plants that bloom on hillsides have adapted to these conditions, just as those that flourish on grass verges have adapted to cope with car fumes or discarded litter. Some plants are survivors but, unfortunately, others are becoming rare due to intensive farming and thoughtless people. It is useful to know if a plant (which has a common and botanical name) is native or non-native. Native flowers have always grown in a country, while non-native plants have been introduced to a country by accident or by gardeners. Plant guidebooks often list plants as either native or non-native.

A meadow filled with a variety of grasses and wild flowers.

Gather common wild flowers for a pretty bouquet.

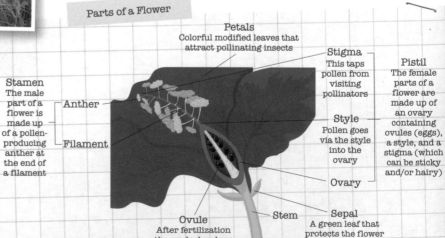

Parts of a Flower

Stamen
The male part of a flower is made up of a pollen-producing anther at the end of a filament

Anther

Filament

Petals
Colorful modified leaves that attract pollinating insects

Stigma
This taps pollen from visiting pollinators

Style
Pollen goes via the style into the ovary

Ovary

Pistil
The female parts of a flower are made up of an ovary containing ovules (eggs), a style, and a stigma (which can be sticky and/or hairy)

Ovule
After fertilization the ovule develops into a seed

Stem

Sepal
A green leaf that protects the flower (a group of sepals is called a calyx)

Make Potpourri

Dry some scented flower petals or herbs in a warm dry place such as an airing cupboard, on the back of a range cooker, or on top of a boiler. Use the petals and herbs as potpourri or pop them into a small fabric bag. Scented bags can be used to perfume a linen cupboard and drawers (see *No-sew Seaweed Bath Sacks*, on page 91 to find out how to make them). Sometimes potpourri becomes damp. If this happens, pop the basket or dish of potpourri somewhere warm until it is dry again.

Rose petal potpourri

What is Pollination?

Flowers are pollinated when insects visit plants to guzzle the nectar and are brushed with pollen. Pollen is produced by anthers (the male part of the flower) and sticks to the insects as they fly from plant to plant. This is how many flowers reproduce and is why bees and other flying insects are so important (see page 17). These insects are called pollinators. The pollen from Miss Poppy (see *Fun Flower and Stick People*, on page 52) has to be carried by an insect to another poppy to make seeds. This is called cross-pollination. Pollen from Miss Poppy can only pollinate another poppy. Pineapple weed (*Matricaria discoidea*), for example, may be growing nearby, but poppy pollen and pineapple weed pollen don't mix—nature is very clever. Pollen can also be carried by animals, wind, and water. Some plants, mostly in the Tropics, are pollinated by birds and bats, but these plants have to produce lots of nectar to keep the pollinators happy. Once pollinated, a flower develops into a fruit—apples, conkers, and hazelnuts are all fruiting bodies.

Keep a Flower Diary

If you are interested in botany (the science of plants), then you might like to keep a diary of the wild flowers you spot when out exploring. Use your diary as a reference to look back on and share your findings with naturalist friends, just as the Reverend Gilbert White did in *The Natural History of Selborne* (see page 11). Each year you'll be able to compare annual differences—for example, a cold spring will delay the appearance of flowers, while a warm spring will hasten this on. Here are a few useful tips to help you get started:

* Note where you see the flower.

* Draw the flower in bud, when open, and after it has seeded.

* Date each stage of the flower's development.

* Record the weather conditions.

* See if the flower's petals close on a dull day.

* Look for pollen on an anther—use some tape to remove a little and stick the pollen in your diary.

* Take photographs and stick them in your diary.

* Add pressed flowers and leaves to your diary.

* Pop back at the same time the following year and write up your diary again—are the flowering and seeding dates the same?

Fun Flower and Stick People

Flower fairies and stick wizards are very easy to make. Just let your imagination lead your wild people designs. Here are some ideas for you to try:

MAKE A FLOWER FAIRY Tie a bunch of flowers to a stick and attach fern or fir wings. Name the fairy after the flowers you used.

MAKE A TEASEL WIZARD Teasels (*Dipsacus fullonum*) grow in damp ground and can become very tall. The spiky flower heads of teasels were used by the textile industry to comb or "tease" out the fibers in fabrics. The Romans called the teasel *Lavacrum veneris*—basin of Venus—because the leaves are joined at the base and fill with water after rain, like a cup. Indeed, if you look closely into the leaves of teasel after a shower of heavy rain, you may see tiny insects that have drowned in a teasel swimming pool. Bees and butterflies visit teasels for nectar and its thousands of seeds are enjoyed by birds.

If you cut off the thorns and are wary of the purple, conical, and prickly flower head, teasels make brilliant stick people. Little else is required because the flower becomes the head, the central stalk acts as the body, and the leaves look like a frilly petticoat. Bravely push a couple of berries into the head to create two eyes, and you have a member of the Teasel family. You could also make a mini den in the woods for your teasel family (see page 35). While in the woods, you might like to craft some fir cones into people and animals (e.g. owls and penguins), or you can make fir-cone fairies to hang on Christmas trees. Acorns are also perfectly sized for crafting into Lilliputian people.

Poppy Power

In L. Frank Baum's children's book *The Wonderful Wizard of Oz* (published in 1900), the magical poppy fields cause Dorothy to fall asleep. Indeed, poppies have long been a symbol of both sleep and death. Sadly, there aren't as many poppies as there once were because, like many corn field flowers, they have been killed by herbicide use. Poppy seeds, however, will lie dormant in the soil, waiting for the ground to be disturbed to encourage new growth. This is what happened during World War One (1914–1918): poppies grew in the fields where the soil was disturbed by battle. The redness of the poppy was also captured by the French artist Claude Monet in his painting *Coquelicots* (Poppy Field).

Make Miss Poppy

You can make a flower fairy without even picking the flower. A common poppy (*Papaver rhoeas*) flower is perfect for this, because the papery petals are flexible and the seedhead creates a perfect head. Carefully push the petals down to reveal the seedhead. Tie a blade of grass or piece of thread from your wild knapsack (see page 8) around the center of the fallen petals so that it looks like a belt. Poke a very thin, short corn stick (which is thinner than a toothpick/cocktail stick) through the petals above the belt of Miss Poppy's torso. The stick will act as the arms and, hey presto, you have a Miss Poppy. Miss Poppy will remain wild as she stands upright on her stalk and sways in the breeze.

Play Grass Games

Grasses are very important for feeding animals and as cereal crops. Some grasses are beautiful. You can dry and press grasses, as well as flowers and seaweed, to make greetings cards and pictures. If you arrange flowers in vases, then why not add some grasses too? Here are some fun games to play with a simple blade or two of grass.

WHISTLE WITH A BLADE OF GRASS

Different widths and thicknesses of grass will produce different whistle tones. Experiment with various grasses and reeds to see which makes the best whistle. Pick a wide and thick blade of grass, but remember never to pick grass near pets and animals (in case it's been in contact with animal waste).

1. Lay the grass the length of the outside of one thumb.

2. Slowly press the other thumb from the base of your hand up to make a small pocket between your thumbs with the blade of grass firmly in between. It needs to be taut (not slack), without any kinks in the grass.

3. Purse your lips (by making a small hole in your mouth) and blow—you should hear a whistle.

4. You can change the pitch of the whistle by moving or cupping your right hand to let air in and out. Be patient: if at first you don't succeed, try again. This is a reed instrument, not a whistle.

CHANT A FALSE OATS RHYME

There are various species of false oats grass (*Arrhenatherum elatius*), but any seeded grass will do for playing this rhyming game. Chant the rhyme: "*Here's a tree in summer, here's a tree in winter, here's a bunch of flowers, and here's an April shower*" as you perform the following actions:

1. Hold the grass—the tree in summer.

2. Run your finger and thumb up the grass to remove the seeds—the tree in winter.

3. Hold the seeds between your finger and thumb—the bunch of flowers.

4. Throw the seeds up in the air to fall on a friend—the April shower.

You can also try blowing through a slit in the blade of grass.

Make Nettle Cordage

The stems of stinging nettles are very tough and strong, which makes them ideal for making wild string or cordage. Nettles can be found nearly everywhere, especially in wastelands and other neglected places. Remember to wear gloves when handling stinging nettles. Pop your finished nettle cordage in your wild knapsack, as you never know when it will prove useful. You might like to use the nettles you have left over after making cordage in your wild kitchen—perhaps in some pesto (see page 29).

WHAT TO USE

- ✔ Pair of gardening gloves
- ✔ Scissors
- ✔ 3–4 stinging nettles (*Urtica dioica*)
- ✔ Small stone
- ✔ Bowl of water
- ✔ Sturdy twig (for storing the cordage)

WHAT TO DO

1. Put on the gloves and cut some nettles with the scissors. (If you are in the garden, and have asked your parents' permission, pull the nettles up by the roots.)

2. Rub the nettles up and down with your gloved hands to remove the leaves and tiny hairs from the stems.

3. Lay the first nettle stem on a garden table or on the ground, and use the stone to flatten the stalk. The best place to bash the stalk is on its knobbly nodes.

4. Remove the woody, yellow center from the stem and throw this away. Repeat this process for the other nettle stems.

5. Keep the outer fibers and leave them to dry in the sun or indoors. The nettle fibers will shrink as they dry.

6. Soak the dry nettle strands in a bowl of water until they're damp. Take two of the strands and lay them out flat. Find a friend and give them one end of the two strands, while you take the other end. You both need to twiddle the strands in opposite directions between your index finger and thumb to create a single piece of string or cordage.

7. Decide at the start which person is going to twiddle to the left and which person to the right. You can add to the thickness of the cordage by twiddling more strands of nettle together.

8. Tie a knot in both ends of the nettle cordage and wrap it around the twig until needed.

Press Wild Flowers and Grasses

Dried and pressed flowers and grasses can be used in craft projects or to build up a herbarium (a collection of preserved plants). A flower press can be useful for pressing flowers and grasses, but heavy books and blotting paper work just as well. Remember only to pick and press common flowers from areas where there are lots of flowers growing and not protected flowers such as cowslips (*Primula veris*).

WHAT TO USE

- Lots of heavy books
- 2 x letter size (A4) sheets of blotting paper
- Selection of wild flowers, leaves, pretty herbs, or grasses (freshly picked for good color retention and as dry as possible)
- Pair of tweezers

WHAT TO DO

1. Open a big book and lay a sheet of blotting paper on one page.

2. Carefully place the flowers, leaves, herbs, or grasses on the blotting paper, so that they are flat, but not touching each other.

3. Use the tweezers to position the petals and leaves so that they will flatten evenly.

4. Gently place the second sheet of blotting paper on top of the specimens and close the book.

5. Put the book in a place where it won't be disturbed and rest heavy books on top. Forget about the flowers for at least three weeks and, if you can, wait four weeks before you take a peep.

6. Remove the books and lift out the pressed flowers, leaves, herbs, or grasses.

Flowers for Pressing

Buttercup (*Ranunculus* spp.)
Chickweed (*Stellaria media*)
Clover (*Trifolium* spp.)
Daisy (*Bellis perennis*)
Forget-me-not (*Myosotis* spp.)
Horsetail (*Equisetum* spp.)
Lesser celandine (*Ranunculus ficaria*)
Marsh marigold (*Caltha palustris*)
Ragged Robin (*Lychnis flos-cuculi*)
Red and white campion
(*Silene dioica* and *Silene latfolia*)
Ribwort plantain (*Plantago lanceolata*)
Rosa rugosa and dog rose petals
(*Rosa canina*)
Shepherd's purse
(*Capsella bursa-pastoris*)
Silverweed (*Argentina anserina*)
Speedwell (*Veronica* spp.)
Sweet violet (*Viola odorata*)
Wood and sheep sorrel
(*Oxalis acetosella* and *Rumex acetosella*)

Mounting Your Work

You can now glue your pressed flowers, leaves, herbs, or grasses to greetings cards, postcards, or pictures, or perhaps add them to your herbarium.

A Handful of Wild Flowers and Herbs

Collecting and classifying plants—and learning the skills of taxonomy (how scientists class species)—isn't as easy as it once was because lots of species are protected. You can, however, use a phone to take photographs, which 19th-century children couldn't do. You can also download apps to help with I.D. You must not pick rare flowers—there are lots of beautiful common flowers to pick and study instead.

CREEPING THISTLE (*Cirsium arvense*) The nectar of creeping thistle, which is a member of the Asteraceae family like the daisy, is loved by butterflies and bees. It is, however, regarded as a pest by gardeners and farmers because it produces a large number of seeds. You will sometimes see the pappus (soft seedheads) of *Cirsium arvense* floating in the air in the late summer and early fall (autumn) breeze (see *Seed Dispersal*, on page 60). You can pick the fluff when it is still attached to the thistle head and add it to a bird-feeding garland (see the *Wild Bird Garland*, on pages 62–63), or use the fluffy balls to paint with. The seedheads are so soft you could soak one in edible berry juices and paint a friend's face. Earlier in summer, the purple creeping thistle is delicately scented.

Make a Daisy Chain

Find a daisy patch and pick some daisies. Use your thumb to make a small slit in the stem of a daisy. Slip the stalk of another daisy through the slit and gently pull the second daisy through. Repeat with another daisy until you have created a chain. Finish the circle by making a second slit in the daisy you started with and pulling through the last daisy stem. You can also try this idea with clover or other soft-stemmed flowers.

Make Flower Jewelry

You can use the purple flowers of creeping thistle to make a bracelet or necklace. Use scissors to cut at least 20 creeping thistle flower heads (you'll need more for a necklace). When you get home, remove any spiky thorns from the flower heads with tweezers. Use a needle with a large eye and some green tapestry thread or yarn to sew through the black base of each flower head to make a chain. Tie the ends of the threads together and you have pretty bracelet or necklace.

You may prefer to use a meadowland flower called knapweed (*Centaurea nigra*) instead. This also has purple flowers but, unlike creeping thistle, it doesn't have spiky thorns. Another idea for making a bracelet is to wrap some sticky tape, with the sticky side facing out, around your wrist and be creative on a walk: stop, pick, and stick flowers to your wild bracelet.

PRIMROSES AND VIOLETS The scented yellow primrose with its crumpled leaves was the favorite flower of British Prime Minister Benjamin Disraeli. Queen Victoria sent a primrose wreath to his funeral on April 19, 1881. April 19 became known as Primrose Day. Primroses grow on banks, in ditches, and in hedgerows, where the pale yellow flower can hide from the sun. Often sweet violets (*Viola odorata*) are found in these places too. The violet hides its flower behind a heart-shaped leaf. In the United States, the violet is the state flower of Rhode Island, Illinois, New Jersey, and Wisconsin. In the United Kingdom, children traditionally gathered primroses and violets as a Mothering Sunday gift. The author Mark Twain wrote of the violet: "*Forgiveness is the fragrance that the violet sheds on the heel that has crushed it.*"

RED CAMPION (*Silene dioica*) This pink flower brightens up hedgerows from spring to summer. There is also a white campion (*Silene latifolia*), which produces a lovely scent at night that attracts moths. Red campion is pollinated by daytime bees and butterflies and white campion, which opens its flowers at night, by night-pollinating visitors.

RAGGED ROBIN (*Lychnis flos-cuculi*) Preferring damper ground than red campion, this plant is invasive in some areas. Its species name *flos-cuculi* means cuckooflower because it flowers (as does lady's smock, see page 118) at the same time as the first cuckoos arrive in the United Kingdom from North Africa.

SCABIOUS The purple-blue flowers of devil's bit scabious (*Succisa pratensis*) and blue-violet flowers of field scabious (*Knautia arvensis*) attract butterflies and bumblebees. The flowers, which look like little pincushions, bloom through the summer and add varied shades of blue and purple to a wild flower garden. Scabious is related to teasel, which can be used to make a stick person (see page 52). The word scabious doesn't sound very nice—it reminds me of a scabbed knee from a playground fall. In fact, the flower was given its name because it was thought to heal scabies (a scabby skin disease). Perhaps my scabbed knee isn't such a silly thought after all.

BURDOCK (*Arctium minus*) This plant grows by roadsides and in fields. In the days before people had refrigerators, the leaves were used to wrap up butter. Some wild cooks like to dig up burdock roots to use in the kitchen, while dandelion and burdock syrup is a favorite children's drink. Burdock seedheads have tiny hooks that catch in the coats of passing animals and on sweaters. You can have fun picking these prickly burs (which are actually seeds) and sticking them on friends. (In fact, the inventor of Velcro fastening got the idea from burdock burs—they stick so well.) In Queensferry, near Edinburgh, there is a festival on the second Friday in August, where a man is clad from head to toe in burdock burs. He parades around the streets chanting: "Hip, hip hurray, it's the burry man's day." People give the burry man money to buy a bur to bring them good luck. Some people buy a bur and stick it back on the burry man because they don't want bad luck. Superstition surrounds this historical event, which is said to keep evil away.

Sorrel Sherbet

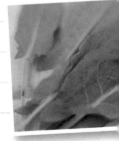

Although sorrel tastes sour, you can add sugar to the ground leaves to make a wild sherbet. Cut a small basket of sheep sorrel (*Rumex acetosella*) leaves. You don't need the stalks. Rinse the leaves and pat them dry. Lay the leaves so they don't touch each other in a food dehydrator or on a baking tray in a very low oven. Finely grind the dried leaves in a liquidizer. Put the ground sorrel in an airtight container. Sift a little confectioners' (icing) sugar into a bowl. Put 1 tablespoon of the sugar and 1 tablespoon of the sorrel in the liquidizer and use the pulse button to blend them together. Tap the sides to knock the sherbet to the bottom and slowly tip the sherbet into a ramekin. Dip your finger in the sherbet and lick the sweet-and-sour wildness.

HONEYSUCKLE (*Lonicera periclymenum*) Moths are attracted to the sweet scent of honeysuckle or woodbind, as country people sometimes call it. Honeysuckle has trumpet-shaped flowers that vary in color, from white to yellow to red. Honeysuckle winds itself around other plants and, given a chance, will spread rapidly through a hedgerow. It also winds down cliff faces at the seaside. William Morris (1834–1896), the British textile designer, wove honeysuckle into some of his wallpapers and other designs. Its curvy stems are ideal for making wild crowns and head-dresses.

RED CLOVER (*Trifolium pratense*) Clover can carpet large areas of wasteland and meadowland. Visiting butterflies and bumblebees are attracted

to red and white clover flowers because both are rich in nectar. Alsike clover (*Trifolium hybridum*) is a mixed-up clover that is either white or pink at the tip with a darker pink flush at the base of the flower. The word hybrid means a crossbreed. Alsike clover can be an invasive species.

Red clover

CLEAVERS (*Galium aparine*) Common in hedgerows and at the edges of fields, the tiny hooks of cleavers will stick to passing animals and clothing. The small, rounded, green fruits are often called sticky Willy or sticky Bob. Wound round in a crown, however, they make a fine wild head-dress—no sticky tape is necessary.

HEDGEROW GARLIC (*Alliaria petiolata*), or Jack by the hedge, grows under hedges since it likes shade. It is a common plant and a bit of a groupie—if you spy one plant, there will be a carpet of them nearby, especially on wasteland. Crush one of its coarse, heart-shaped leaves and you'll smell garlic. The tiny white flowers appear from mid-spring to early summer. Hedgerow garlic has a milder flavor than wild garlic but, nevertheless, is a useful herb in the kitchen—you can use it instead of wild garlic or nettle leaves to make *Wild Garlic Pesto* (see page 29).

SHEPHERD'S PURSE (*Capsella bursa-pastoris*), a member of the cabbage family, is another wasteland fan. It's easy to identify by its heart- or purse-shaped fruits. The peppery leaves taste great in salads and, like sheep sorrel (see page 148), are an early spring green.

Make a Honeysuckle Crown

Cut a length of honeysuckle that will fit around your head, loop it, and then secure the circle with some string, if you need to. Often a double honeysuckle circle can be twisted to make a crown without the need for string. Pop other flowers into the circle if you wish. If you want to keep biting insects away, then add some sweet gale or bog myrtle (*Myrica gale*). You can also dry sweet gale and use it to scent drawers.

Sweet gale

Sticky cleavers

Common Meadow and Hedgerow Plants

Traditionally, grass was allowed to grow through spring and summer, and cut between mid-summer and Lammas Day (August 1). It was then grazed until late fall (autumn). This farming practice provided an amazing diversity of wild flowers for pollinators. There aren't as many hedgerows and meadows today, but (with permission) you could change the mowing pattern of your garden lawn and start your own mini wild meadow. Make a note of the flowers and wildlife that visit. Perhaps you will find a rare flower, like a cowslip.

Sheep sorrel

Blackberries

Buttercup

Violets

Hedgerow garlic

Scabious

Chickweed

Seeds and Fruits

In the summer you can have fun competing with birds to fill a small basket with fruits. Wild strawberries and raspberries are the perfect size for snacking on as you walk along. In the fall (autumn), you can gather seeds and nuts. Snacking aside, the fall is about dispersing seeds from the parent plant to avoid overcrowding and competition for food and water.

SEED DISPERSAL

Seeds are dispersed (carried away) from the parent plant in many different ways. Some seeds known as burs, such as those of burdock (see page 57), have tiny hooks that attach themselves to the coats of passing animals. Other seeds like dandelions and thistledown are blown by the wind. Their delicate seeds are sometimes seen floating in the air in late summer and early fall (autumn). These seeds are sometimes referred to as a pappus. The pappus of common groundsel (*Senecio vulgaris*), which grows almost anywhere, are fairy-sized in comparison to those of creeping thistle (see page 56). Groundsel's botanical name makes good sense—*vulgaris* means "common." The seeds of some plants, including poppies and members of the broom tribe (Genisteae), are stored in a seedpod, which is blown by the wind or floats downstream in rivers before bursting open to release its seeds. On hot summer days, listen out for the popping of gorse and vetch seedpods.

Other seeds are enclosed in the soft-bodied berries of hedgerow plants. In summer, you'll find wild gooseberries, raspberries, and bilberries. As the days shorten in fall, blackberries, sea buckthorn (*Hippophae rhamnoides*), and elderberries (*Sambucus nigra*) appear. There are recipes that use some of these berries in *My Wild Garden and Kitchen*, on pages 148, 152, and 154).

Animals and birds scatter seeds and nuts as they move about. They also disperse indigestible seeds (especially those encased in berries) in their droppings. Birds enjoy pecking out the seeds of the slightly harder cased hips and haws too (see the *Bird-feeding Roll*, on pages 132–33). There are many species of wild roses and they all have different hips. The hips of the dog rose (*Rosa canina*), for instance, are oval and tiny compared with the fat, mini-tomato-like hips of *Rosa rugosa*. It is easier to forage big, fat hips. You can use seedless hip and haw flesh in a jelly or fruit leather (see page 148). Rosehips are good for you because they contain lots of Vitamin C.

Some wild fruits have stones called drupes. In late-summer hedgerows you may find wild cherries and damsons (*Prunus domestica insititia*), which are sour plums. In the fall, sloes—the fruit of the blackthorn (*Prunus spinosa*)—make a welcome appearance.

Know Your Berries

It is important that you know how to identify any berries you come across when exploring the countryside. This is because some berries are poisonous. Young naturalists need to be "berry clever" and understand that eating certain berries, such as those of yew (*Taxus baccata*), can be fatal.

HAVE FUN WITH SEEDS

You can use the different seeds you come across in meadows and hedgerows in outdoor activities and games, as well as craft projects. Here are a few ideas to start you off:

WATCH A PLANT SET SEED Spring is the start of the growing season, which for a plant begins with a seed. This is a good time for young naturalists to choose a plant and follow its life cycle as the seasons pass. Find a germinated seedling, visit the spot regularly with a notepad and pencil, and keep a record of how the seedling develops into a new plant before producing seed of its own.

TIME-TELLING WITH A DANDELION CLOCK First find your seeded dandelion (*Taraxacum officinale*) and then blow. Count the puffs—counting an hour for each puff and blow until all the seed has blown away. Dandelion clocks tell different times to different children. Some children will blow hard, others will blow gently, and what of the wind? Sometimes it helps with time-keeping too. When you blow on a dandelion clock, you're helping nature by spreading the seeds. In spring, try adding young dandelion leaves to salads.

MAKE A WILD BLING BRACELET You can thread different seeds onto a short length of shirring elastic to make a wild bling bracelet. Older children can use a skewer to make a hole through the middle of some acorns or small conkers, and thread these onto the elastic. Alternatively, simply tie the elastic around some little alder cones.

MAKE ROSEHIP ITCHING POWDER

In France rosehips are called *gratte-cul* or "scratch your arse," which is rather rude. Scottish children call rosehips Itchy Coos. Beware of playing this trick on friends with allergies or sensitive skins.

Collect some ripe rosehips, snapping off the leaves and prickly stalks as you pick. Wear some gardening gloves to do this. Wash the hips and then put them onto a tray lined with paper. Dry the berries in a warm, airy place for two weeks until they are wrinkly and hard. You can also dry the hips in a low oven or food-dehydrator if you wish. Cut open the shriveled berries and take out the fine hairs—these are your itching powder. You can keep the leftover seeds for wild cooking or feed them to the birds. Store your itching powder in an airtight jar or envelope. Then, let the itching begin—sprinkle some itching powder down the back of a friend's neck.

You can also make itching powder from whirlygigs or maple seeds. Gently rub two maple seeds together over a sheet of paper and tiny hairs will fall onto the paper. Store this itching paper in a small pot or envelope.

Make a
Poppy Seed Necklace

Poppy seeds ripen in a dry fruit capsule. This fruit is perfect for threading onto a length of colored shirring elastic to make a pretty wild necklace. Nature has given the poppy fruit or pistil (the female part of the flower) a very interesting shape and its top is colored with a glint of gold—no paint spray is required. In the wild, if the poppy fruit is left to grow, the seeds float away in the breeze from tiny holes at the top of the seedhead.

Wild Bird Garland

This simple garland is easily adapted to suit the season and you can use whatever is in the store cupboard. Some people like to thread popcorn and dried fruits on a garland to decorate their Christmas tree—you can do this with wild edibles too. The birds will appreciate your hard work as they snack on the garland on a cold day after Christmas. For a free and really wild garland, get outside and forage seeds and berries, instead of raiding the kitchen store cupboard. If you have a fir tree in the garden, this is perfect for draping a garland over, but a bush will do just as well. The birds aren't fussy. You can make your garland as short or long as you like, although the longer the garland, the greater the number of wild edibles you'll need to forage.

WHAT TO USE

- ✔ 78in (200cm) strong embroidery floss (thread) or 39in (100cm) thin craft string or cordage (see *Make Nettle Cordage*, on page 54)
- ✔ Tapestry needle (with a large eye)
- ✔ Collection of small bowls
- ✔ Selection of wild haws, hips, seeds, thistledown, and small cones (such as alder cones)
- ✔ Ready-to-eat popcorn (air- not oil-popped, so it is not greasy)
- ✔ Dried fruit
- ✔ Fresh cranberries, blueberries, and blackberries (as in season and not over-ripe)

WHAT TO DO

1. Thread the embroidery floss or craft string through the tapestry needle. If you are using embroidery floss, then double up the thread. (If you are using thicker string or nettle cordage, use the tapestry needle or a small screwdriver to make a hole very carefully in the berry etc., and thread without using a needle.)

2. Put each of the ingredients in a separate bowl to make it easier to choose what to thread onto your garland next.

3. Thread the first ingredient and then use the end of the thread or string to tie a knot around the wild edible to make an anchor. You will need to twist the thread around the small cones (or groups of cones).

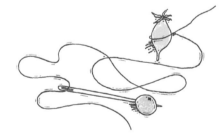

4. Continue threading the wild and store-cupboard ingredients onto the embroidery floss or string. Try to create a colorful pattern as you thread. Make sure you don't use anything too soft and squishy or too thick (e.g. nuts), which can make the task tricky and messy.

5. When you have finished, tie a knot around your last ingredient. If you want to make a longer garland, then leave a length of floss or string to tie the next garland on to. Hang your garland outside and watch the birds as they come to feed.

Wild Seasonal Tip

Lay the berries and hips you have collected on an open tray and put this in the freezer. Pack the frozen edibles in plastic bags and label them clearly: *For The Birds*. You can use the berries throughout the year.

Feed the Birds

Birds' tastes vary just as our favorite foods differ. Most berries are red or black, which makes them easy for birds to find. Some birds such as starlings feed in flocks, but the mistle thrush (*Turdus viscivorus*) likes to eat alone. Finches prefer seeds from alder cones, while thrushes prefer berries with tiny seeds, such as those of the rowan, because they really only want to eat the berry flesh.

Do some research and find out what different species like feeding on and then plan your bird garland menu with this in mind. Size is important too. Large dog rose hips, for example, are probably best for blackbirds, but won't attract smaller birds. Berries are also attractive to insects and in late summer butterflies will also flutter toward syrupy fruits.

Spring Nest-building Depot to Entice Birds

In spring, when birds are building their nests, hang wild and household bits and bobs over the garland. You could use sheep wool, feathers, hair from your hairbrush, mosses, lichen, twigs, animal fur, straw, grasses, strips of newspaper, scraps of material, yarn, and string. Watch as the birds peck and pick things up and fly away to use in nest-building. It is very easy for humans to put something on a garland, but a tiny bird has to fly to the garland, pick out its chosen nesting material, and then fly back to its nest site. If they are sensible, the birds will come back to their ready-made nest-building depot—what lucky birds.

Inks and Dyes

Not so long ago, all dyes and paints were made from natural ingredients. The added fun of a wild berry moustache is that you can lick it clean. Berry paints change color as they dry: some colors fade, while others don't. Artwork is enjoyable with natural pigments, but it is very unpredictable—it's tricky to repeat the recipe for a magical color, but this is part of the experimental fun.

WILD INKS AND FACE PAINTS

Each season brings new wild ink colors. Historically there have been lots of uses for natural inks, such as making cosmetics and coloring pottery. Our ancestors decorated cave walls with natural colors, although some of these came from minerals, not plants. Some dyes also came from shellfish and insects. In the Roman Empire, the purple dye murex came from several kinds of sea snail called Muricidae. Lots of snails were needed to dye fabric Tyrian or Imperial purple, so purple clothes were a luxury that only the rich could afford. The red coloring cochineal is made from an insect (a member of the Dactylopius family).

MAKE HUCK FINN'S WILD INK You can easily use mud for war paint, but any wild edible berry that stains is tastier. You'll probably have a good idea of which berries to use from foraging—just look at your hands. Choose berries that are ripe. Bilberries (*Vaccinium myrtillus*)—known as huckleberries in the USA—produce a purple/red ink but actually write in blue, while raspberries are great for writing in pink. Put three level tablespoons of bilberries or raspberries and one teaspoon of water in a small saucepan. Cover the pan with a lid and cook the berries over a low heat for 5–7 minutes until they collapse. You may need to add a little more water to stop the berries sticking to the pan. Leave the berries to cool. Push the berries through a small plastic sieve into a small glass jar. You will now have very thick ink. You can add a few drops of seawater or salted tap water if the ink is too thick (when cooled), but don't add too much. Store the ink in the refrigerator. The ink won't last very long, so... grab some paper, dip your writing utensil into your natural ink, and start writing or drawing—you won't find a bottle of this in stores. You could use bivalve shells collected from the beach as wild ink containers.

TURN BLUEBELLS PINK Acid can alter wild ink colors. In spring, find an ant nest and put a slightly squished Spanish bluebell (*Hyacinthoides hispanica*) on top. The ants will investigate and spray a jet of formic acid on the bluebell. Wait and see what happens—the bluebell will turn into a pinkbell. This change is due to the flower's blue pigment anthocyanin being exposed to acid. You could also try this experiment with garden lobelia.

NATURAL DYES

Dyeing with lichens and other wild plants is experimental, but great fun. At times it can also be a little messy. Wild colors will vary according to the time of year, as well as which plants are in season, or, in the case of lichens, where they have been picked. Always wash dyed garments separately.

Picking raspberries

USING LICHEN You can use wild lichen for dyeing projects, but not in cookery recipes—this is because lichen tastes bitter. The Isle of Harris in the Outer Hebrides, in Scotland, is famous for its tweed, which is used on some Nike products. Tweed colors were originally made from dyes using local plants and lichens. Hebrideans call *Xanthoria* lichens by the general Gaelic name of *crotal*. To be precise, the word refers to the dyes, not the lichen. Harris Tweed mirrors the colors of the Harris landscape because the wool was dyed using local plants. In the past, dyeing wool was usually the job of women and children who also collected the lichen from rocks on the hills and by the sea. Lichens may look drab, but when material has been layered with lichen and boiled in water—ideally rainwater—it turns rich bronzes, yellows, and purples.

Dyeing with lichen is rather like cooking. Good cooks add and subtract ingredients, and experiment with cooking times, as their confidence grows. You can do this with wild color dyeing too. There are many lichens in various colors: some may be dull gray, while others (like *Xanthoria parietina*) are almost orange. Orange lichen will, with luck, dye a purple color. Black lichen (*Xanthoria omphalodes*) is an easy dye to start with because, like other lichens, it doesn't need a mordant to "tie in" the color (or make it colorfast). The word mordant comes from the Latin word *mordeo*, which means "to bite" or "take hold of"—so a mordant fixes the dye to the fabric. Dyes that don't need a mordant are called substantive dyes—the dye color won't wash out.

COLLECTING LICHEN Use an old spoon to scrape lichen from rocks on damp, windless days. Scrape a little here and there into a container and then pop on the lid. It is more difficult to remove lichen on sunny days because the heat dries it onto the rocks. You can also dye with old man's beard or Spanish moss (*Tillandsia usneoides*), which can be found growing on trees and even on fence posts.

Plant and Berry Dyes

Here is a short list of plants to use in color experiments. You can also make dye colors using mushrooms (see *Studying Fungus Spores*, on page 43). When you forage wild ingredients to use as natural dyes, only pick a small amount and never more than one-sixth of any plant or berry. Chemical dyes have now replaced natural dyes, which is a good thing because otherwise we would strip our countryside of wild plants and berries. The dye color you can expect from each plant is given too.

Berries

Bilberries (*Vaccinium myrtillus*)	Purple/red
Blackberries (*Rubus fruticosus*)	Purple
Damsons (*Prunus domestica insititia*)	Purple/blue
Elderberries (*Sambucus nigra*)	Purple/blue
Sea buckthorn (*Hippophae rhamnoides*)	Yellow/orange
Sloes (*Prunus spinosa*)	Purple

Flowers

Bog myrtle (*Myrica gale*)	Yellow
Dandelions (*Taraxacum officinale*)	Yellow
Gorse (*Ulex* spp.)	Yellow
Ragweed (*Ambrosia* spp.)	Yellow
Rosa rugosa	Pink

Leaves and roots

Nettles (*Urtica dioica*)	Olive-green
Sheep sorrel (*Rumex acetosella*)	Red (roots) and green (leaves)

Lichens — Brown/yellow/purple

Seaweed

Dulse (*Palmaria palmata*)	Brown

What is Lichen?

Together some alga and fungus create an organism called lichen. They are dependent on each other for survival. Deserts and Arctic and Antarctic regions are rich in lichens, which can thrive in hot and cold temperatures. Lichens are a diverse group; they come in lots of shapes and sizes and grow very slowly. Some lichen grow like crusts (Crustose)—look on tombstones. Others look like dry leaves (Foliose) and some resemble mini trees with lots of hair (Fruticose). Lichenologists (who study lichen) use a microscope to I.D. lichens, but you can look at them with your magnifying glass. The photograph above shows some different lichens, including the bushy-looking old man's beard (*Usnea* spp.), growing on a rock.

DYEING FABRICS Collect a plant or berry to dye your piece of fabric (see *Plant and Berry Dyes*, on page 65). You'll also need a suitable mordant such as vinegar or salt because, unlike lichens, most plants and berries need a mordant to fix the dye. Vinegar is used to fix plant dyes and salt is used to fix berry dyes. (If you live by the sea you can use seawater as a mordant for berry dyes.) There are different methods for adding the mordant, but the rose and blackberry dyeing recipes given here prepare the fabric by using the mordant first. Experimenting with plant and berry dyes and mordants is part of the fun—just like a natural chemistry lesson. Practice dyeing little cotton squares with small quantities of plants and water, and keep a cooking pot with a lid for your experiments.

Rose-dyed handkerchief

WHAT TO USE

- ✔ 1¾oz (50g) *Rosa rugosa* petals from a hedgerow (shaken to remove any insects)
- ✔ Saucepan
- ✔ Rainwater
- ✔ Potato masher
- ✔ Sieve
- ✔ Bowl
- ✔ *For the mordant to fix the color:* ¼ cup (50ml) vinegar and ¾ cup (200ml) water
- ✔ Shallow dish
- ✔ Small handkerchief

WHAT TO DO

1. Put the petals in a saucepan and cover with rainwater. Put the pan on the stovetop and bring to the boil (lots of bubbles). Lower the heat to a simmer (small bubbles) and cook for about 2 hours until the petals are white, not pink. Gently bash the petals with the potato masher and leave to cool.

2. Strain the pink rose water through the sieve into the bowl. Squeeze the petals to remove all of the rose water.

3. To make the mordant, mix the vinegar and water in the shallow dish and soak the handkerchief for 30 minutes. Squeeze out as much of the liquid as you can and then pop the handkerchief into the rose dye.

4. Leave the handkerchief soaking in the dye for as long as you want. Leave overnight for a bright pink handkerchief, less time for a paler pink.

5. Wring the dye from the handkerchief and hang out to dry on a washing line.

Blackberry-dyed handkerchief

WHAT TO USE

- ✔ ¾ cup (100g) blackberries from a hedgerow (shaken to remove any insects)
- ✔ ⅓ cup (100ml) rainwater
- ✔ Saucepan
- ✔ Potato masher
- ✔ Sieve
- ✔ Bowl
- ✔ *For the mordant to fix the color:* ⅓ cup (100ml) water and 1 teaspoon (5g) salt
- ✔ Spoon
- ✔ Shallow dish
- ✔ Small handkerchief

WHAT TO DO

1. Put the blackberries and rainwater in the saucepan and cook over a low heat for about 5–10 minutes until the blackberries have collapsed. Gently bash the blackberries with the potato masher and then leave the mixture to cool.

2. Strain the blackberry juice through the sieve into the bowl.

3. To make the mordant, use the spoon to stir and dissolve the salt in the water (make sure you use enough water to cover the handkerchief) in the shallow dish.

4. Soak the handkerchief in the salt water for about 20 minutes.

5. Squeeze out as much liquid as you can and pop the handkerchief into the blackberry dye.

6. Leave the handkerchief soaking in the dye for as long as you want. Leave overnight if you want a bright red handkerchief.

7. Wring the dye from the handkerchief and hang out to dry on a washing line.

Old-man's-beard-dyed handkerchief

WHAT TO USE

- ✔ 3 handfuls of old man's beard/Spanish moss (*Tillandsia usneoides*), which usually dyes dark orange/brown
- ✔ Small handkerchief
- ✔ 2 cups (500ml) rainwater
- ✔ Small saucepan

WHAT TO DO

1. You don't need a mordant to fix the dye when you use old man's beard. Put the old man's beard, handkerchief, and rainwater in the saucepan and cook on the stovetop over a low heat for at least 1 hour (longer if you want a darker color).

2. Leave the handkerchief to cool in the dye, then wring out and hang on a washing line to dry.

Wild Color Diary

Keeping a wild color diary will help you to learn about natural dyes. The weather, season, and location, as well as the type of water and cooking pot—large, stainless-steel pots are best—will all affect the color of the dye. Write notes on:

- ✳ The weather, place, and date that you picked the plant or berry.

- ✳ The fabric you used—natural fabrics such as silk, cotton, and wool work best.

- ✳ How much of the plant or berry, as well as water, you used.

- ✳ How long you cooked/left the material in the dye.

- ✳ How much mordant you used.

- ✳ Stick a color swatch (tester strip) of your dyed fabrics in your diary.

World of Insects

Entomology is the study of insects. Entomology developed quickly in the 19th and 20th centuries because there are millions of species of insects to catalog. In the *Autocrat of the Breakfast Table*, the American academic and poet Oliver Wendell Holmes Sr. (1809–1894) wrote: *"No man can be truly called an entomologist, sir; the subject is too vast for any single human intelligence to grasp."*

FASCINATING INSECTS

Like plants, insects have evolved by adapting to the habitat in which they live and there is a number of them to learn about. They vary in size, from tiny fairyflies, which are the smallest insects in the world (about the size of a period or full-stop), to the giant weta, a cricket-like creature found only on Little Barrier Island, New Zealand. This is the world's largest insect, with a wingspan of 7in (18cm).

Adult insects have a head, thorax (mid-body), and a lower abdomen (body), antennae for smelling, two large compound eyes, and three pairs of jointed legs. Antennae are very important because an insect's sense of smell is vital to its survival. It uses its antennae to find food and sniff out enemies (predators). Dragonflies use their legs to hold their food and eat on the move. This is really cool—it could be called flying fast-food.

Insects are cold-blooded, which means that their growth depends on temperature (i.e. how hot or cold it is). They have developed lots of tactics to survive the winter. They may hibernate (sleep), become dormant, or hide in plant galls (swellings). Some insects group together before going into hibernation. As an insect's temperature lowers, its body processes slow down. Honeybees keep warm by clustering together inside a hive, while ladybugs (ladybirds) spend winter in a dormant state (they stop growing) and wake up in spring when it gets warm again.

Ladybugs

You probably know what the ladybug (ladybird) *Coccinellidae* looks like because of her stunning, spotted, red coat, but there are lots of different types of ladybugs. Become a ladybug spotter. Lady refers to the Virgin Mary (Our Lady), who in early paintings often wears a red cloak. Farmers and gardeners like ladybugs because they feed on the pests that damage crops and vegetables. Sometimes ladybugs are bred to help farmers and smallholders control aphids (greenfly) and other soft-bodied insects.

SOME COMMON INSECTS

There are enough insects to fill many books. If you're interested in a particular type of insect, then it's a good idea to research them online or read specialist books. Here are a few common insects:

BEES Some species of bees, including bumblebees and honeybees, are very sociable and like living in large colonies. Different groups of bees have different work to do. There are female workers and male drones, and a Queen who is responsible for laying the eggs that develop into drones and workers. Honeybees have been domesticated for thousands of years, making it easier for us to gather honey. A United Kingdom brand of golden syrup has an illustration of a lion surrounded by bees on the can. This tells the bible story of Samson, who kills a lion and returns to find a swarm of bees and a honeycomb—so we read of wild honey in biblical times. Beekeepers keep bees in hives with removable frames. The bees store honey in the upper frames, which the beekeeper removes to collect the delicious honey. Bees are invaluable pollinators of crops and wild flowers too (see page 17).

Bees do a special dance (called a waggle dance) to communicate with their hive mates and tell them the best places to forage food. Scientists have done some rescarch on this dance. They studied:

✽ The angle of the dance in relation to the sun.

✽ The length of time the bee waggled its abdomen while moving in a figure-of-eight pattern.

From this information, researchers have mapped the locations where bees forage, as well as the distances they travel, from month to month.

GRASSHOPPERS Entomologists and ecologists (people who study all organisms and where they live) are interested in grasshoppers because they are in competition with man for food. They are herbivores (eat grass) and sometimes eat so much that crops are ruined. This can be a problem for poorer countries. Grasshoppers are similar to their close relatives, the katydid and cricket. They

Build an Insect Hotel

You can build a hotel for insects in any secret, well-camouflaged place. Visit regularly—just like a hotel inspector—but remember that this inspection is a top naturalist secret. Some of your detective work may well be underground. Take some spoons, a magnifying glass, and your pocket I.D. book, notebook, and pencil.

are green or brown and change color with the season to blend into their environment. In some parts of the world, grasshoppers are considered delicious to eat. There are three main types of grasshopper: long-horned, short-horned, and pygmy. Thousands of different grasshopper species can be found living in meadows, fields, and woods. Listen out for their mating call.

There are four key stages in a grasshopper's metamorphosis: egg, wingless nymph, winged nymph, and adult. The grasshopper wriggles out of its old skin, emerging with a new skin that has grown underneath. This is called molting—the shedding of the hard exoskeleton (a skeleton outside of the body). Humans have an endoskeleton (inside of the body). The grasshopper molts a number of times as it grows. After it has molted (i.e. it is in a soft new exoskeleton or larger skin), the grasshopper remains motionless until its body has hardened. You can learn a a great deal from watching insects.

Caterpillar

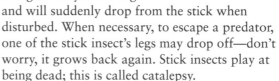

MOTHS AND BUTTERFLIES also undergo metamorphosis, moving through four stages: egg, caterpillar, chrysalis, and adult moth or butterfly. A good guidebook will tell you where you are most likely to find different species. Hidden in the Latin name for the large white butterfly (*Pieris brassicae)* is the reason that gardeners don't like its caterpillar. This common butterfly is often called the cabbage (*brassica*) butterfly because it likes eating cabbages. There are lots of species to note if you keep a butterfly diary. Don't just search for rare species because common butterflies are often overlooked and so under-recorded. You could use a special net to look very closely at butterflies or conduct *After Dark Moth Investigations* (see page 145).

Small white butterfly
(*Pieris rapae*)

STICK INSECTS Some children like to keep a stick insect as a pet. These insects cling to trees, shrubs, and sticks (which is where their name comes from). Stick insects camouflage themselves well and are most active at night. They eat foliage and will suddenly drop from the stick when disturbed. When necessary, to escape a predator, one of the stick insect's legs may drop off—don't worry, it grows back again. Stick insects play at being dead; this is called catalepsy.

ANTS Some species of insects such as ants are burly workmen; they can carry things many times their own weight. Sometimes ants work together, which means that they are able to drag huge objects. Army ants are carnivorous and as a team can kill and eat worms and small vertebrates. Ants are very organized. In their homes (anthills) there is a series of tunnels, with each area having a specific purpose (e.g. a larder or resting place). Not all ants live in anthills, however. Army ants carry their food and young with them and move around like nomads. An ant has two tummies: one for its own food and a second called the crop where it keeps food for sharing. Each colony has a special scent which helps ants recognize each other.

Ants clash with rival ant groups. The winner of an ant war is usually the army of ants with the largest colony. Birds sometimes peck ants and drop them on their feathers. They do this because the ants spray formic acid which kills any bugs on the feathers. This very cool medical wildlife partnership is called anting. If you are looking closely at ants, please beware: ants bite.

Encourage ants
with some sugar.

Ant Experiments
for Young Naturalists

You might like to try these interesting ant experiments. They will give you an opportunity to study how ants behave and interact with each other.

HOW DO ANTS BEHAVE?

WHAT TO USE

- ✔ Teaspoon
- ✔ 4 live ants
- ✔ Clean glass jar with a lid
- ✔ Small screwdriver (for putting holes in the lid)
- ✔ Moist greenery (such as dandelion or chickweed leaves)
- ✔ Sugar
- ✔ Magnifying glass

WHAT TO DO

1. Use a teaspoon to collect 4 live ants (from the same area and hopefully the same colony) and pop them in the glass jar. Put on the lid. Make sure you have put holes in the lid using the screwdriver.

2. Tilt the jar, add some greenery, and put a pinch of sugar down one side of the jar. Replace the lid and leave the jar on its side. What do the ants do?

3. Observe the ants using the magnifying glass and ask yourself questions such as:

   ✳ Do the ants use their feelers to touch each other?

   ✳ How do the ants behave as individuals and as a group?

4. Visit your glass jar after dark to see what happens when you turn on a light. Do ants rest?

5. Release the ants when you have jotted down your observations.

WHAT DO ANTS LIKE TO EAT?

WHAT TO USE

Ant Menu One
- ✔ Cake or cookie (biscuit) crumbs
- ✔ Sugar
- ✔ Small cubes of carrot
- ✔ Shredded dandelion leaf

Ant Menu Two
- ✔ Selection of candies (such as jelly beans) with grape, apple, strawberry, orange, blackcurrant, lime, and lemon flavors

Ant Menu Three
- ✔ Red, orange, blue, green, yellow, pink, violet, and brown colored candies (of the same variety)

WHAT TO DO

1. Scatter the food from *Menu One* in piles in an area where there is ant activity.

2. Wait patiently and see what the ants choose to eat.

3. Place the colored candies from *Menu Two* in a different area and again wait for the ants to choose their food. The candies are flavored—does this influence the ants' food choice?

4. Repeat Step 3 for *Menu Three*. The results of this experiment will tell you whether ants have a food color preference.

3 Seashore

The seaboard of the world can take many forms, including soft, sandy beaches, rugged and rocky seashores, and magnificent coral reefs, but these coastlines have all been sculpted by the mighty power of the sea. A walk along your local beach will give you a real sense of the effect that the rhythm of the sea has had on its cliffs and rocks. The life of a sea cave, for example, begins when powerful waves find a weakness and force out a hole. Once formed, a sea cave creates shelter for sea life and the possibility of sea adventure for young explorers accompanied by adults. The seashore is indeed a wonderful place to explore and discover the natural world, whether you want to learn about oceans and tides or the amazing world of seaweeds and how to use them in crafts and cooking. The beach is also a great place just to have fun paddling, shell-seeking, and rock-pooling.

Oceans and Tides

Sometimes the sea is glassy and calm, while at other times it is stormier, roaring and tossing white-horse waves out at sea and pounding crashing waves onto the seashore. Human beings don't have any power over the sea, but the forces of the Sun and Moon do.

THE TIDE RISES, THE TIDE FALLS

If you're busy building sandcastles on the beach on a sunny, windless day, it's easy to forget about the movement of the sea. Unfortunately, the tide doesn't wait for sandcastle builders. On most coastlines, twice a day, the oceans rise to cover the beach (high tide) and fall (low tide) to uncover a wonderful ocean garden.

The area of land covered between high and low tide is known as the tidal range. This twice-daily ebb and flow, which is called a semi-diurnal tide, is caused by the gravitational pull of the Sun and Moon. Some areas, like the Gulf of Mexico, have one low and one high tide each day. This is called a daily or diurnal tide. The tides of the Mediterranean are tiny; you may not even notice them, because they are less than a few feet high, but the tides of the Pacific and Atlantic Oceans are huge. The Isle of Wight, in England, has double tides known as Double High Water. This means that there are four of each a day. The highest tides in the world are in the area of the Bay of Fundy in Nova Scotia. In the United Kingdom, the Bristol Channel boasts the world's second largest tidal range.

The Sea in Mythology

The Roman sea god was called Neptune. He was temperamental and the Romans believed that his moods reflected the ever-changing moods of the sea. Sometimes he was grumpy, at other times joyous and fun. A merman known as Triton pops up in Greek mythology. Triton had a human upper body and a fish's tail. He carried a conch shell, which he blew to calm the sea under the direction of his father, the sea god Poseidon.

Big tides, which cover all of the seashore with seawater and then retreat far, far away, are called spring tides. These happen every two weeks when the Earth, Sun, and Moon are in line during a new or full Moon. Smaller tides form when the Sun, Earth, and Moon are at a right angle and the Sun and Moon pull the sea in different directions. This means that when the tide is out (low tide), it isn't far to walk to the sea and at high tide, the sea doesn't swallow up all of the seashore, leaving you beach to play on. These tides are called neap tides and happen during a quarter- or three-quarter moon. I call them sluggish or lazy tides.

The time between low and high tides varies each day because the tidal cycle is 50 minutes longer than our 24-hour day. When there are two daily tides, high and low tide are 6 hours, 12½ minutes apart. If you work out the mathematics, this adds up to 24 hours and 50 minutes. Keeping an eye on the tide is very important for safety reasons.

Watch the Tides

Keeping an eye on the tide is very important for safety reasons.

Spring and Neap Tides

Tides occur due to the gravitational pull of the Sun and Moon on the oceans. Spring tides happen when the Earth, Sun, and Moon are in line during a new or full moon, while neap tides take place when the Sun and Moon pull the sea in different directions when the Moon is waxing or waning. (To learn more about the phases of the Moon, see page 144.)

Big spring tides have higher high tides, which cover most of the seashore, and lower low tides that reveal the subtidal zone. A sluggish neap high tide doesn't cover all of the beach and a low neap tide doesn't expose as much of the ocean floor.

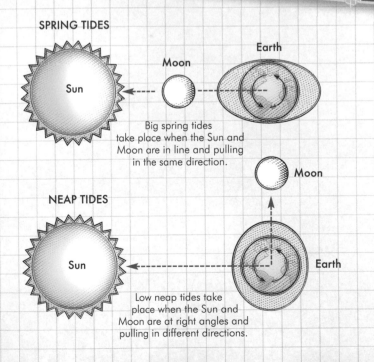

SPRING TIDES

Sun · Moon · Earth

Big spring tides take place when the Sun and Moon are in line and pulling in the same direction.

NEAP TIDES

Sun · Moon · Earth

Low neap tides take place when the Sun and Moon are at right angles and pulling in different directions.

SEASHORE ZONES

The seashore is divided into three separate zones (which you can see in the photograph opposite). Each zone is home to the different seaweeds and sea creatures that have adapted to the conditions there.

THE SPLASH ZONE is the area of beach that is usually dry unless there is a big spring tide. Seawater splashes grass and rocks during a high spring tide. This is why this part of the seashore is called the splash zone. The seaweeds that grow here often look black, and feel dry and brittle, but they can survive for long periods out of seawater.

THE INTERTIDAL ZONE is covered by the sea at high tide and revealed at low tide. The sand here is usually damp unless it is a very hot day. Sometimes there are pools of water, in spite of the tide being out. This is the perfect habitat for lots of sea life. The seaweeds that you find here can tolerate some sunshine, but not too much. Barnacles, cockles, and mussels also live in the intertidal zone. If you have a fishing net, then you can have fun exploring the rock pools (see page 100) in this zone. Have a good look at any sea life in your net and remember to put it back where you found it. The sea life that lives in the intertidal range appears and disappears according to the changing nature of its world. This happens the world over, wherever the land meets the sea.

THE SUBTIDAL ZONE Sub means underneath, so this area of the seashore is almost always covered by seawater (it's revealed at a low spring tide). When there is a big (spring) tide the water will be shallow and you can paddle out and explore sea life. The big, strong brown kelp seaweeds live here. Their crooked holdfasts look like the roots of an old tree and the fronds will wrap around you as you paddle. Red seaweeds contain a pigment that allows them to grow as deep down as light can penetrate the seawater; you'll find lots of these seaweeds in this zone.

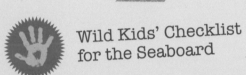

Wild Kids' Checklist for the Seaboard

Where Land and Sea Meet

The ocean garden is pretty, but it can be dangerous too. Bear the following in mind when you're out beachcombing:

* **Check** the tide times and watch out for odd local tides (e.g. double tides).
* **Check** the weather forecast. Strong winds can hurry tides along.
* **Always** explore the seashore with a friend and have adults close by.
* **Wear** non-slip footwear. Bare feet have a good grip in summer, but beware of weever fish that hide in sand in shallow water. They have sharp spines and can cause painful injuries to bare feet.
* **Carry** a warm sweater and phone in a knapsack.
* **Check** the route back as you go. The tide can sneak in when you are behind a rock.
* **Beware** of sinking mud estuaries, where you may become stranded.

Tidal Zones

Seashores are divided into three zones: the splash zone, the intertidal zone, and the subtidal zone. The varying conditions in these zones (e.g. the length of time that the area is under water and exposed to sunlight) will influence the types of seaweed and sea creatures that can exist there.

THE SUBTIDAL ZONE

THE SPLASH ZONE

Periwinkles

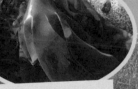

Seaweeds

THE INTERTIDAL ZONE

Limpets

Starfish

Crab

Mussels

Seaweed on the Seashore

Marine algae is the name for plants that grow in the seas, as well as in some sea lakes. *Marine* is the Latin word for "sea" and *algae* means "seaweeds." There are thousands of different seaweeds. *Micro* means "small"—you won't be able to see *microalgae* in the water because they are tiny, floating, one-cell beings. *Macroalgae* or seaweeds are bigger (*macro* means "big"). The kelps, for example, are huge and can carpet the floor of the sea like a dense forest, so it isn't surprising that there's a member of the kelp family called forest kelp.

Parts of a Seaweed

Blade

Frond

Stipe

Holdfast

Thallus

WHAT IS SEAWEED?

Seaweeds are not plants because they don't have roots. Instead, they anchor themselves using a holdfast. A kelp holdfast looks like the roots of an old tree. A holdfast may be attached to a rock, pebble, shell, flotsam and jetsam (marine words for wrecks and trash), another seaweed, or even a manmade bridge. A holdfast is a fabulous and complex habitat—and may be home to lots of different species. Seaweeds also have a stipe, which is like a plant stalk, and a blade similar to a plant's leaf. A collection of blades is called a frond and a seaweed's body is called a thallus. Seaweed growth responds to the length of the day (i.e. to sunlight levels). Some seaweeds have air bladders (see page 83), either alone or in pairs depending on the species.

Marine scientists who study seaweed are called phycologists, a word that comes from the Greek word for seaweed. Phycologists divide seaweeds into three color groups: red, green, and brown. The color of a seaweed is a result of the different mixtures of pigments (the brown, green, and red colorings) that it contains. All seaweeds have green pigments so they can make energy from the sun. This means that seaweeds are producers because they provide solar (sun) energy. The food chain (see opposite) always starts with a producer, so seaweed is at the bottom of the food chain. Seaweeds provide food and shelter for lots of sea life, and are an important part of our human food chain, but we still have a great deal to learn about these amazing organisms.

Seashore Food Chains

Seashore Food Chains

Snails eat seaweed, crabs eat snails, and some people like eating crabs. This is an example of a food chain. Plankton, which like seaweed is at the bottom of a food chain, is eaten by barnacles—these are consumed by dog whelks, which may then be eaten by a herring gull.

Top Consumers
(e.g. Humans)

We get our energy
from producers
and consumers.

Secondary Consumers
(e.g. Birds)

These get their energy
from primary consumers.

Primary Consumers
(e.g. Mollusks
and Arthropods)

These get their energy
from eating seaweed.

Primary Producers
(e.g. Seaweed and Plankton)

The seaweed's energy
comes from the sun.

FINDING AND IDENTIFYING SEAWEEDS

Individual seaweed species are very different, even though they are collectively called seaweed. So, it's a good idea to take a pocket seashore guide to the beach so that you can look up the names of seaweeds as you find them. There are thousands of seaweeds to learn about and marine biologists need a microscope to identify some of them. The longer you spend looking for different species, the more seaweeds you will spot. Seaweeds like rocky shores because they can anchor their holdfasts to pebbles and rocks.

The neighborhood or habitat in which a seaweed lives is chosen because it suits the seaweed. Some types of seaweed grow near the top of the beach; some live in the middle of the beach, where they are uncovered by the sea at low tide; and others prefer to be covered by seawater all of the time, even at low tide. Certain seaweeds prefer a sheltered beach, while others enjoy the rough and tumble of the open sea. The kelps like cold water and channel wrack chooses to be out of the water for long periods of time. The more time you spend on the beach studying where seaweeds grow, the more you will understand why a type of seaweed grows where it does. There are over 10,000 species of seaweed worldwide. Here are some common seaweeds to look out for:

CARRAGEEN (*Chondrus crispus*) **AND GRAPE PIP WEED** (*Mastocarpus stellatus*) are red seaweeds that can be found at low tide hanging from rocks or carpeting pebbles. It is rare to find carrageen out of the water except at low tide. If you are exploring rock pools, you will probably come across carrageen. Use a pair of scissors to cut its tiny stipes from the rock, but leave plenty to encourage regrowth. Grape pip weed is also called carrageen. It isn't smooth like *Chondrus crispus*, but bristly and usually covered in bubbly warts. Carrageen is used as a setting agent in toothpaste and ice cream, and also helps to make the froth on beer.

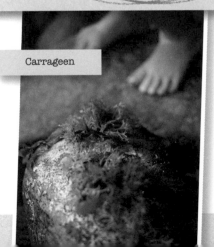

Carrageen

DULSE (*Palmaria palmata*) is a red seaweed that you'll find growing on rocks and other seaweeds. It looks like a hand with short fingers and this may be where its botanical name, *Palma*, comes from. Dulse has a long history of being useful to man and is probably one of the oldest foods eaten by coastal people in times of hardship. St. Columba and the monks who brought Christianity to Scotland made a soup using dulse which they'd gathered on the shores of the Isle of Iona.

Green sea grass, red dulse, and brown forest kelp

PEPPER DULSE (*Osmundea pinnatifida*) is no relation to dulse (*Palmaria palmata*), although it is a member of the red seaweed group. Pepper dulse has a very small frond that looks like a small fern. It can vary in color, from ruby red to brown, and has a garlic-like taste. It's tricky to harvest because it is tiny and reduces in volume when dried. Fortunately, pepper dulse has a strong flavor, which means that a little goes a long way when you cook with it. Chefs like cooking with pepper dulse—you should try it too.

LAVER (*Porphyra* spp.) is called nori by the Japanese who consider it to be a delicacy. They grow nori and use it in sushi. Laver or nori is a red seaweed, although it may look green, brown, or even black. Its botanical name is *Porphyra* spp. (When you see the abbreviation spp., it means there is more than one variety within that genus.) It took a long time for scientists to understand the life cycle of this seaweed. Until 1949, when a British scientist called Dr Kathleen Drew made a very important discovery about laver, it was thought that it was not one but two seaweeds. If laver is put under a microscope, it looks different during the various stages of its life cycle. You will find laver on rocks in the intertidal zone. Laver can survive the wind and being out of seawater. It clings tightly to the rock as it dries and you will need to be eagle-eyed to spot it. Cut laver with scissors as the tide is coming in. The laver floats with the incoming tide and the seawater helps to wash the sand away too. Laver is used to make traditional Welsh laverbread.

Dulse growing as an epiphyte on kelp

Harvesting laver

Sea lettuce

SEA LETTUCE (*Ulva lactuca*) looks like common-or-garden round lettuce. There are, however, lots of species of this look-alike green seaweed and they are tricky to identify correctly. Gutweed (*Ulva intestinalis*), which I prefer to call mermaid's hair, is a tubular, worm-like seaweed. Its Latin name is easily translated to intestines or guts.

Mermaid's hair likes the upper shore, where it often begins life growing on a small shell and then, with time, it will carpet large areas of the beach. Sea lettuce, mermaid's hair, and other similar green seaweeds are often grouped together as *Ulva* spp. These seaweeds like growing where fresh water flows into the sea—but don't pick them here. Instead, cut sea lettuce from rock pools, where there is no worry of contamination from human waste. Sea lettuce is sometimes called green nori because it looks like thick, green laver or nori. Laver and sea lettuce both have tiny stipes, so make sure you cut them carefully with scissors and leave enough seaweed to allow regrowth.

SEA SPAGHETTI OR THONG WEED (*Himanthalia elongata*) looks like wheat spaghetti and, like lots of seaweeds, changes color when cooked—it turns green when you pop it in boiling water. Its species name, *elongata*, means "long" and its fronds often float like tresses in seawater. It attaches itself to rocks with a button-like base. Don't cut these buttons or the seaweed won't grow again. You will find thong weed at low tide, often carpeting islands of rocks when the tide is out. Try cooking washed thong weed with wheat pasta—it will add some sea vegetables to your plate.

Sea spaghetti

Sea spaghetti looks like wheat spaghetti and, like lots of seaweeds, it changes color when used in cooking

THE KELPS, such as oar weed and forest kelp, are very orderly, but you will only see them at low spring tide. Closest to the beach is the shiny, brown seaweed called oar weed (*Laminaria digitata*). The stipe of oar weed is oval in cross-section, smooth, and flexible. It is also usually free of epiphytes (other seaweeds growing on it). Forest kelp (*Laminaria hyperborea*) looks similar, but its stipe is usually longer and thicker, and it is circular when cut in half. As you go deeper out to sea—you may, in fact, need a wet suit—oar weed is replaced by forest kelp. This seaweed has a rough stipe on which other seaweeds like to grow (as an epiphyte). The red seaweed dulse (*Palmaria palmata*) often grows on forest kelp.

Sugar kelp (*Saccharina latissima*) seaweed is sometimes known as poor man's weather vane because people use it to forecast the weather. Whether the sugar kelp is brittle or damp is said to depend on the amount of moisture in the air—damp seaweed forecasts rain. This seaweed is often covered in a sweet white powder called mannitol, which is used by doctors in some hospital treatments.

Furbelows (*Saccorhiza polyschides*) is easy to identify because it has a splendid frilly stipe. Its brown frond is rather ragged and unruly at the edges. Neat people might want to trim it with a pair of scissors. Furbelows' claw-like holdfast is fat and warty. You might think that its stipe would make a good belt, and you'd be right because it certainly looks like one.

Sugar kelp

Sea grass

Knotted wrack

THE WRACKS As you go down to the sea, the first seaweed you will see is channel wrack (*Pelvetia canaliculata*). Sometimes this looks brittle and black because it can spend days out of the water. Also look out for bladder wrack (*Fucus vesiculosus*), with its paired air bladders (which help some seaweeds to float so that they can receive more sunlight). Bladder wrack has fewer bladders on exposed shores than when it grows in sheltered bays. Serrated wrack (*Fucus serratus*) has a midrib (a thick stalk down the middle) and saw-like edges, but no bladders. Serrated wrack is used by beauticians. If you cut some and take it home, rinse it well and then wash with it at bath time. Knotted wrack (*Ascophyllum nodosum*) can live for 15–20 years and its bladders may become very large. It can compete with bladder wrack for space, but knotted wrack doesn't like rough seas— it will only invade bladder wrack's territory when there isn't much wave action. Count the bladders on knotted wrack and have fun guessing its age—it is said to produce one bladder per frond each year.

Furbelows

Wracks

Bladder wrack

Ulva species

Knotted wrack

Carrageen

Kelp

Seaweed Spotter's Guide

When you are walking along the beach or having fun in the waves, see how many types of seaweed you can spot. Different seaweeds flourish in different areas of the seashore. For example, channel wrack prefers the drier conditions at the top of the beach, while others, like the kelps, thrive in the sea.

Sea spaghetti

Laver

Furbelows

Dulse

Seaweed—and its Amazing Uses

Macroalgae is a really useful weed. You can pop seaweed in the bath, cook with it, or use it in craftwork. Plan a visit to a herbarium, where you will be able to see beautifully preserved plants and seaweeds—our ocean flowers—and find out the best ways to preserve a seaweed's shape and color.

COLLECTING, DRYING, AND STORING

If you are not planning to use your seaweed fresh from the seashore, then it can easily be dried and stored for using in recipes or other projects later on.

Collecting Seaweed

There are a few rules to bear in mind when collecting seaweed from the seashore for use at home:

* **Don't** pick storm-cast seaweed for cooking; only use seaweed that is growing.
* **Do** use a pair of scissors to cut seaweeds from their holdfasts at low tide on a clean beach. (Remember to take scissors with you when you visit the beach.)
* **Don't** cook with floating seaweed or seaweed that grows at the top of the shore near drains. Sea lettuce and sea grass like growing here—instead, pick these seaweeds from rock pools at low tide.
* **Do** wash the seaweed in the sea so that any hidden "visitors" can find a new home locally. You should also rinse the seaweed in cold water when you get home.
* **Do** use a separate bag for each type collected, as this will make it easier to sort out your seaweeds when you get home.

DRYING SEAWEED When you get home, wash the seaweed thoroughly. Rinse it in cold water and squeeze out as much of the water as possible. A salad spinner is helpful here—spin the seaweed around, just as you would if preparing salad leaves. Next dry the seaweed. Lay the pieces of seaweed on a tray lined with newspaper or some paper towel—making sure that they aren't touching—and leave to dry on a sunny windowsill. You could also pop the tray in a warm airing cupboard. On a sunny day, you can dry larger seaweeds such as sugar kelp by pegging them on a washing line. You can also dry seaweed on trays in a low oven or even in a food dehydrator if you have one. Some people dry seaweed in a hot oven, but you *must* be eagle-eyed if you do this and make sure that the seaweed does not burn.

Dried dulse

Dried dulse

Dried laver

Dried sea lettuce

STORING SEAWEED When you have dried the seaweed, cut it into manageable lengths or grind it in a food-blender. It is easier to grind a little at a time, pop it in an airtight container, and then repeat the process until you have used up all of the seaweed. Shake the containers when you remember and use the dried seaweed as a flavoring, just as you would herbs or spices.

COOKING WITH SEAWEED

Seaweed has been a part of coastal diets for hundreds of years. The Japanese have cooked with seaweed for centuries, but cooks have recently started adding seaweed to British and American recipes. Although it is fun to forage for seaweed on the beach, it is becoming increasingly available in some stores.

Dried laver, sea lettuce, mermaid's hair, carrageen, dulse, and sugar kelp are very handy for wild cooks. You can pick these seaweeds at low tide, wash and dry them, and then use them in recipes. You can also cook with fresh seaweed. Chopped fresh dulse and sugar kelp both cook within 20–25 minutes and sea spaghetti can be boiled or steamed in 10–15 minutes. Finely chopped seaweeds (species of *Ulva* are ideal) can be stir-fried for fast food and thin, round fronds such as laver and sea lettuce may be used as a protective wrapping on barbecues, or in the oven (instead of baking parchment).

COOKING SEA SPAGHETTI Put the sea spaghetti in a saucepan of boiling water and cook for about 15 minutes, depending on how thick the fronds are and how soft you like your spaghetti. You may wish to eat your sea spaghetti *al dente*; if so cook it for 10 minutes, but leave it for longer if you prefer it softer. As it cooks, the sea spaghetti will change color from brown to emerald green. Try mixing this green sea vegetable with some cooked wheat pasta and serving it with your favorite pasta sauce.

There are some seaweed recipes in *My Wild Garden and Kitchen*, so have a go at making a *Seashore Omelet* (see page 156), some *Seaside Sprinkles* (see page 155), or some *Dulse and Cheese Scones* (see page 155).

Pick seaweeds at low tide, wash and dry them, and then use them in recipes

Seashore Omelet

Other Ingredients to Pick by the Seashore

The flowers and seashore edibles that survive by the sea have adapted to the sand dunes, shingle beaches, salt marshes, and mud flats where they grow. For example, some seashore plants have thick leaves to protect them from the salt, wind, and sand.

Marsh samphire (*Salicornia* spp.) is sometimes called glasswort. It grows on rather dirty-looking sand called mudflats. Since it has roots, it is classified as a plant, not a seaweed. It may look like an emerald-green Jurassic cactus, but this delicious green vegetable bursts with seaside juices when you bite into it. Try adding some raw marsh samphire to egg sandwiches (but make sure you wash it well first). Glasswort contains a lot of soda and has been used since biblical times for making soap and glass. It was imported into the United Kingdom from the Mediterranean under the name of barilla. John Josselyn, a 17th-century English traveler, who wrote about his travels in New England, USA, mentions glasswort (which he calls *berrelia*) as a New England rarity. Don't muddle this plant with rock samphire, a member of the carrot family.

Rock samphire (*Crithmum maritimum*) has an interesting lemony taste and smells like floor polish when you bruise it. Its yellow-cream flowers attract lots of insects. Some people like the taste of rock samphire leaves, while others hate it. Remember that you must never eat any wild plant unless an adult has helped you to identify it correctly. William Shakespeare referred to collecting rock samphire as a dreadful trade because the poor harvesters had to hang from coastal cliffs in order to pick the plants—it certainly was a dangerous occupation.

Orache (*Atriplex* spp.) is part of the goosefoot family and likes growing by the sea. You can pick these plants in sand dunes and on salt marshes from early summer through to early fall (autumn). They taste like spinach, but it is quite tricky to identify between species. Some species are frosted—their leaves look as if they have been sprinkled with a fine layer of confectioners' (icing) sugar. Other orache species have spear-shaped leaves. You can use orache in any recipe that asks you to include spinach.

Pasta and Marsh Samphire

For a quick and delicious supper, add a couple of handfuls of marsh samphire to a saucepan of pasta for the last 3 minutes of cooking time. Drain well and return the pasta and marsh samphire to the pan. Add a small can of salmon, some cream or yogurt, and a splash of lemon juice, and supper is ready. You can, of course, use fresh salmon instead or, even better, go fishing and see if you can catch your own fish. Pick samphire soon after Midsummer's Day, if possible, because it gets woody with age. Although you can still eat it, you'll need to cut out the tougher stalks.

CRAFTING WITH SEAWEED

Seaweed is beautiful. Some species are fragile, while others feel leathery and slippery when wet. A seaweed known as velvet horn (*Codium tomentosum*) feels like a velvety billiard table. During the reign of Queen Victoria, a seaweed-collecting craze developed in the United Kingdom and North America. Pressing seaweeds is a useful way of preserving them and then you can create your own seaweed library to document the specimens that you've found. Pressed seaweeds can also be used to make pretty greetings cards, postcards, and bookmarks. You can learn how to prepare seaweed specimens on the *Preservation of Natural History Collections* website (see *Resources*, on page 157).

A Simple Method for Mounting Lightweight Seaweeds

Lightweight seaweeds can be mounted to make pretty greetings cards or for your seaweed library. You may like to put the mounted seaweeds into poly-pocket files or in a scrapbook, as 19th-century children did. The first mounting may be a little tricky but, like learning to ride a bicycle, it becomes easier with practice.

WHAT TO USE

- ✔ Scissors
- ✔ Selection of light seaweeds (such as the feathery red *Heterosiphonia plumosa*)
- ✔ Small bowl of cold water
- ✔ Small paintbrush
- ✔ Piece of thick card or paper, measuring 6 x 6in (15 x 15cm)
- ✔ Tweezers or a toothpick
- ✔ Pile of heavy books

WHAT TO DO

1. Use scissors to cut some seaweed at low tide.

2. When you return home, rinse the seaweed and put it in a bowl of cold water to keep cool. Never leave it in a hot place. (If you're busy, you can keep the seaweed in the refrigerator for a day.)

3. Take the seaweed you want to press and use the paintbrush to brush it dry. Use scissors to trim the specimen to fit your piece of card or paper. You can use a larger piece of letter size (A4) card and more fronds if you would like to poly-pocket file your seaweed.

4. Place the seaweed on the piece of card or paper, and use a wet paintbrush to gently position the seaweed. Then use the tweezers or toothpick to arrange the seaweed.

5. Leave the card or paper on a sunny windowsill to dry. Seaweeds contain a sticky substance and so should stick without glue. When the seaweed looks dry, carefully put some heavy books on top of the card or paper and leave for a further 2–3 weeks.

6. Label the card or paper with the seaweed's species, as well as the date and place you picked it.

BATHING WITH SEAWEED

Bathing in seaweed has a long history as a cure for diseases and as a soothing dressing. The Maori people who live in New Zealand used seaweed on cuts and wounds, and today it is used in some types of hospital dressing to treat wounds. In early-20th-century Ireland, there were over 300 seaweed baths along the coastline, where people suffering from aches and pains would go to bathe. Some still exist today and seaweed is often used in spa treatments. Many shampoos and beauty lotions contain carrageen, one of the wracks (*Fucus* spp.), or kelp. Beauty product manufacturers have their own secret seaweed ingredients, but serrated wrack is often on their list.

USE FRESH SEAWEED IN THE BATH

At the beach cut a little serrated wrack and bladder wrack above the holdfast. When you get home, rinse the seaweeds well under running water and then pop them in your bath tub. The seaweed will turn green in hot water and the bath water will change color like a chameleon. Sometimes it turns green; at other times olive brown. Have fun trying to pop the bladders on the bladder wrack as you wash the seaweed's gel onto your skin. Pop the seaweed in a bag after bathing and you'll be able to use it a second time.

Many shampoos and beauty lotions contain carrageen

No-sew Seaweed Bath Sacks

These easy-to-make bags make a lovely seaside vacation memory or gift. Younger children can practice knots as they tie the sacks. Soak the bath sack in your bath water for 5 minutes before you use it, unless, of course, you want to spend a long time in the bath. As the seaweed rehydrates, it releases a gel that has skin-softening properties.

WHAT TO USE

- ✔ Dried seaweed, cut or broken by hand into short lengths
- ✔ Jelly bag, pop sock, or a leg of pantyhose (tights), cut below the knee
- ✔ Ribbon, for tying (optional)

WHAT TO DO

Stuff the dried seaweed into the jelly bag, pop sock, or section of pantyhose and then tie a knot (and a ribbon, if using) tightly at the top to make a sack. You can use colored or patterned pop socks or pantyhose if you wish to make your bath sacks look really pretty.

Summer Wild Rose and Carrageen Soap

Making your own soap is great fun and means you can be sure it only contains natural ingredients. Seaweed can be used in lots of bathing and beauty products. You will enjoy washing up the utensils used to make this soap because the gel from the carrageen feels lovely and soft.

WHAT TO USE

MAKES 1 SMALL JAR OR CONTAINER

- ✔ 2 teaspoons (10g) dried carrageen (see page 87 to find out how to dry seaweed)
- ✔ Bowl
- ✔ Saucepan
- ✔ 1oz (25g) *Rosa rugosa* petals
- ✔ Potato masher
- ✔ Spoon
- ✔ Sieve
- ✔ 5–6 drops red food coloring (optional)
- ✔ Jar or plastic container

WHAT TO DO

1. Put the dried carrageen in a bowl and cover with water for about 10 minutes. When the carrageen has soaked up the water, squeeze it well to remove excess water and pop it in a saucepan.

Carrageen Seaweed

If you are exploring rock pools, you'll probably come across carrageen (see page 79 to discover more about this useful seaweed). Use a pair of scissors to cut its tiny stipes from the rock, but leave plenty to encourage regrowth. You will probably find lots of snails in the carrageen, so wash the seaweed in the sea to allow any visitors to rehouse themselves locally before popping it in a bag.

2. Add the rose petals to the pan and just enough water to cover. Cook over a low heat and simmer for about 30 minutes until the mixture is very, very thick. Mash the mixture with a potato masher every so often to make sure that it doesn't stick to the pan. Remove the pan from the heat and leave to cool for 5 minutes.

3 Spoon the mixture into a sieve over a bowl and use the spoon to push as much of the cold rose and carrageen soap through the sieve as possible. Remove the sieve and stir in the red food coloring if you wish.

4 Put the soap in a small glass jar or plastic container with a secure lid and store in the refrigerator between bath times. Use the soap within 7 to 10 days.

Variation

CUCUMBER AND CARRAGEEN SOAP

You can also make the soap using carrageen and grated cucumber. Follow the recipe and instructions for the *Summer Wild Rose and Carrageen Soap*, but use ½ small cucumber (instead of the *Rosa rugosa* petals) and 4–5 drops of green food coloring (optional). Before adding the cucumber to the pan of carrageen, first grate it into a bowl using the coarse (big) blade of a grater—stop before you reach the end of the cucumber or you may cut yourself. You can also add a handful of wild mint leaves to the mixture to give your soap a mint fragrance. Put the finished soap in a small glass jar or plastic container with a secure lid and store in a refrigerator. Use your soap within 7 to 10 days.

Shells on the Seashore

There is a large variety of arthropods which make up about 85 percent of all the animal species from the land and sea. Mollusks are also a big animal group with different forms and they have very distinct shells. When you're next at the beach, see how many types of shells you can find.

ARTHROPODS

These have an exoskeleton or a hard outer shell to protect them from the outside world. If we forget to use sunscreen, then our skin may peel. Although arthropods don't get sun burnt, they can and do shed their outer shell. They move about with the help of five to seven pairs of jointed legs and two pairs of antennae—what makes them special is that they are segmented. Crustaceans are members of this group, which includes crabs, lobsters, and barnacles—it's a varied gang. Barnacles attach themselves head down to rocks and shells, using a cement gland at the base of their antennae. A barnacle will stay put on the rock or shell (its base) for the rest of its life.

Empty crab shell

MOLLUSKS—THE SHELLMAKERS

The word mollusk comes from the Latin *mollis*, meaning "soft"—mollusks don't have any bones. There are probably over 100,000 types of mollusks, but nobody knows the exact number. Their soft body is covered by an outer layer called a mantle. Most mollusks have shells, but the mantle or cloak of those that don't is often multi-colored. In some species, the mantle cleverly changes color when the mollusk senses danger. This is brilliant camouflage. In most mollusks, however, the mantle is used to make an outer shell or "portable home."

A few mollusks actually have an internal shell, which is sometimes called a bone, but is, in fact, more like a special crystal that traps air. The most well known is the cuttlefish which isn't a fish at all; it is more like a squid.

Mollusks that live in a shell are grouped according to their thick muscle foot and the type of shell in which they live. They make one shell for life, which grows with them. Some mollusks use their foot to clamp themselves to a rock, while others use it to rush about. When you find an empty shell on a beach, it was once home for a soft-bodied mollusk.

Various animals belong in the phylum (see page 11) Mollusca, which has eight divisions or living classes. The biggest contains the gastropods, most of which live in a single coiled shell.

Looking for shells

Bootlace seaweed growing on a razor clam.

GASTROPODS The word gastropod comes from the Greek *gaster*, meaning "stomach," and *podos*, meaning "foot"—gastropods move by foot with a side mouth for snacking. The foot leaves a gummy trail and some mollusks use a radula or bristly, tongue-like organ to scrape for food. The word *radula* comes from the Latin "to scrape." Tiny new teeth grow at the back of the radula and older teeth fall out at the front. Some mollusks have a single radula, while others have thousands of these fangs, which are made from goethite. This is the strongest iron-based mineral known to man. A limpet could eat through a bulletproof jacket if it wished. Some mollusks use their radula as a weapon to hunt or bore into the shells of other mollusks. This is why you sometimes see shells with holes in them. The deadly cone snail, which is found in the South Pacific and Indian Oceans, is a gastropod that can cause paralysis or even death in fish and humans by spitting a nasty poisonous cocktail from its radula.

Gastropods come in all shapes and sizes, with the shape of the animal defining the shell in which grows it. Abalones, whelks, limpets, and periwinkles belong to this group, as do slugs, although these don't have a shell. Slugs that leave a gummy trail in the garden are ocean migrants—their ancestors originally came from the sea.

BIVALVES form the next biggest class of mollusk. They have twin shells or valves held together by a hinge. They close their shells using the powerful muscles near the hinge of the twin shells, which keeps visitors out. Try opening an oyster—it's tricky. Bivalves don't have a radula like gastropods. Instead, they filter tiny food particles from water through feathery gills. Mussels, oysters, cockles, scallops, and clams are all bivalves.

Mussels use a strong (byssal) thread to attach themselves to a solid surface. Oysters also attach themselves to rocks, but by creating a powerful cement. Some scallops lay on their side, cemented to rocks, but scallops are the only bivalves that swim. They move by rapidly opening and closing their shells. Cockles (*Cerastoderma edule*) and common and pod razor clams (*Ensis ensis* and *Ensis siliqua*) live in the sand. I call cockles and clams "the burrowers." As the tides rises, cockles come to the surface or push up breathing tubes to pump water through their underground burrows. They feed on tiny animals and plants in the sand. When the tide goes out, these bivalves push deep into the wet sand so that they don't dry out. Barnacles (which are arthropods, not mollusks) close their shells to keep in as much moisture in as possible, while snails will withdraw into their shell to shut out the dry air.

CEPHALOPODS are the largest of all the mollusks, as well as the most intelligent and mobile. Most of these animals have a small internal shell, so they aren't studied by conchologists (shell collectors). They do, however, have a developed head—*kephale* means "head" in Ancient Greek. Cuttlefishes and various squids and octopuses are members of this group. They have clever tubes for feet which spurt out jets of water and push them through the sea at speed. The shell inside a squid is called a squid pen. Cuttlefish and octopus can change color in the blink of an eye for camouflage or to find a mate—a bit like teenagers blushing when they like each other. Scientists even think that the octopus has a sense of smell. "Cephalopods are clever pods."

Whelk
MOLLUSK
GASTROPOD

Oysters
MOLLUSK
BIVALVE

Limpets
MOLLUSK
GASTROPOD

Crab
ARTHROPOD

Cockles
MOLLUSK
BIVALVE

Barnacles
ARTHROPOD

Periwinkle
MOLLUSK
GASTROPOD

Arthropod and Mollusk Identification

There are thousands of species of soft-bodied mollusks. They include mobile cephalopods, which are clever chameleons, the bivalves whose homes are tricky to burgle, and the snail-like gastropods. Arthropods are everywhere, not just in the sea. Some live on land or in ponds, where they fly, creep, and crawl.

Lobster
ARTHROPOD

Octopus
MOLLUSK
CEPHALOPOD

Squid
MOLLUSK
CEPHALOPOD

Cuttlefish
MOLLUSK
CEPHALOPOD

Mussels
MOLLUSK
BIVALVE

Clams
MOLLUSK
BIVALVE

Scallops
MOLLUSK
BIVALVE

Go Shell-seeking and Rock-pooling

At the beach it's fun to paddle in the shallow waters and look for colorful pebbles and shells, or perhaps some shellfish for supper. Take your fishing net so that you can examine the sea life that thrives in the rock pools—seize your moment because the tide will return and your rock pool will disappear.

THE SHELL-SEEKERS

When you're at the beach, it's fun to search for and examine different types of shells—you'll see more colors and details if you rinse the shells in seawater to make them wet. On my local beach I look for the tiny Hebridean Arctic cowrie shells, *Trivia artica* or *Trivia monacha* (with dark spots on the shell), but these aren't real cowries. The real cowries belong to the Cypraeidae family. They are usually smooth and shiny like porcelain, and many are colorful too. Shells are one of the oldest forms of currency. The *Monetaria moneta*

cowrie shells were taken on long journeys and traded in West Africa—the Ghanaian unit of currency was named after the cowrie shell.

The Native Americans of New England made beads called wampam from shells and these were used as money when European settlers arrived. Abalone shells are stunning. Native Americans ate the abalone meat and then used the whole shells as bowls and smaller pieces to make necklaces. They also bartered with abalone shells.

Take a net to the beach so that you can study different shells in the shallow waters. You may find some tidal treasures such as this lovely cowrie shell (right).

You only have one go at knocking a limpet from its rock, but then you should leave it alone. If you succeed, then examine the muscular foot that the limpet uses to move around as it grazes on seaweed.

The outside of an abalone shell is dull, but inside is a glorious mother-of-pearl—jewelers love these shells.

You may not find a glistening abalone shell on the beach, but limpets (*Patella vulgata*) are very common on rocks and stones. They have a very strong foot, which they use to stick to the rocks. It is said that you have one go at knocking a limpet from its rock and, if you don't succeed, it will be impossible the second time. This is where the expression "to stick like a limpet" comes from. Older boys and girls may try to disprove this theory, but I suggest: one go and, if you miss, leave the limpet alone. The limpet shell protects the limpet as it presses against the rock; it looks like an Asian conical hat. The waves wash over the limpet's shell, but their force cannot move it from the rock. The Greek philosopher Aristotle first noted that limpets leave their places on the rocks at high tide and go out to feed, but that they always return home at low water. Limpets feed on seaweeds by licking them with their radula.

At low tide look out for the tiny, but stunning, blue-rayed limpet (*Patella pellucida*), which feeds on the brown kelp, oar weed (*Laminaria digitata*). This limpet has blue lines on its shell. Other common shells for shell-seekers include the common whelk (*Buccinum undatum*) and common periwinkle (*Littorina littorea*). Common periwinkles are easy to prise from the rocks, but their rounded shape is clever, protecting them from big waves.

Shell-spotter's Fascinating Facts

❋ Conchology is the study of shells and people who do this are called conchologists. The word conchologist comes from *konkhos*, the Ancient Greek word for "cockle." Conchologists usually study four molluskan orders— gastropods, bivalves, and two smaller groups: chitons and tusk shells.

❋ Most coiling shells twirl in the same direction: clockwise to the right. Collectors are always on the look out for shells that coil to the left. Add these to your list of things to spot in the wild, along with four-leaved clovers (most only have three leaves).

❋ The Merman Triton blew on a conch trumpet and a conch shell is used as a symbol of power in William Golding's book *Lord of the Flies*—the rule being that only the boy holding the conch may speak. Conch trumpets were used across the Americas to summon people and spirits. In Hawaii, where the conch is called **Pū**, the meaning of the number of blows is deeply sacred. The shell of the giant triton (*Charonia tritonis*) has a pointed spire in a single shell, so it is a gastropod. It is commonly known as Triton's trumpet.

❋ The internal shell from the cuttlefish (which is a squid-like mollusk) is used by parrots in their cages like a nail file to keep their beaks in trim.

❋ The Roman emperor Caligula found the English Channel so rough that he could not cross it, so he punished Neptune (the god of the sea) by confiscating (collecting) all the shells on the shore—or so the story goes.

EXPLORING ROCK POOLS

When the tide goes out, seawater sometimes becomes trapped in rocks until the tide comes in again. On a sunny day the water in rock pools can become very warm—rock pools are nature's paddling pools. They are exciting places to explore with a fishing net, but make sure that you return sea animals to the pool after you have had a good look at them. Seaweeds cover some rocks but, if you peep underneath, you may find periwinkles, limpets, and whelks hiding. Snails eat seaweed but larger creatures crawl about in rock pools too. Crabs eat snails and, although you won't see the food chain in action, you may see a crab scuttle away if you lift up a small rock. Plant-eating animals are called herbivores. Herbivores are eaten by meat-eaters (e.g. the crab) and these animals are called carnivores. On a hot day rock-pool residents are exposed to the sun but, fortunately, nature is kind and each animal adapts to the heat in its own way. The returning seawater will cover up the rock pool and refresh the sea life, but you'll have to await the next low tide to continue your exploring adventures. The tide waits for no man.

JELLYFISH ALERT You may come across a jellyfish in a rock pool or when swimming in the sea. Jellyfish come in lots of shapes and sizes, but they all have a jelly-like composition; this is where their name comes from. Some are translucent, some glow in the dark, and others are rather pretty. Jellyfish often appear in large groups and this is called a bloom. There can be thousands of jellyfish in a bloom. If a jellyfish is cut in half, it can grow into two new organisms. The problem with jellyfish and human beings is that jellyfish are meanies and use their tentacles to sting. They don't, however, set out to sting humans; we just get in the way—look out for them and you won't get stung. Most of the time a jellyfish sting is nippy but harmless. The sting of the beautiful Portuguese man-of-war (*Physalia physalis*), for example, which was named after an armed 18th-century sailing ship, is painful, but not usually fatal to humans. On a scary note, the stings of some jellyfish species can kill humans—in fact, the venom of the box fish or sea wasp jellyfish (*Chironex fleckeri*) can kill a person in minutes.

Jellyfish

STARFISH You may also be lucky enough to spot a starfish. There are over 2,000 species of starfish or sea stars. Some starfish live in the intertidal zone (see page 76), so you often come across them on the seashore. In spite of their name, they are not fish because they don't have gills, scales, or fins. Starfish are, in fact, echinoderms; their bodies have five sections arranged around a central disk. In common with sea urchins (which are also echinoderms), a starfish feels rather spiky because of the jagged spines that it uses as protection against predators. If a starfish loses an arm, it can regrow (regenerate). This is pretty cool as the starfish can ditch an arm and get away, if it gets into a fight. A starfish moves on hundreds of seawater-filled tubular feet on the underside of its body. Its mouth is on the underside too. To feed, a starfish wraps its arms around mussels or clams, and forces open the shell. What happens next is nature at its best: the starfish pushes its stomach out of its mouth and guzzles the contents of the mollusk. When it's done, the starfish re-swallows its stomach and begins to digest its meal. This is clever as it allows the starfish to eat more than it can fit into its very tiny mouth.

Treating a Jellyfish Sting

If you are stung by a jellyfish, rinse the area with seawater and don't rub the sting. Use a bank card to scrape away any stingers left on the skin. If you do this at home, apply some shaving cream or baking soda (bicarbonate of soda) and seawater mixed into a paste before using the bank card. Avoid using fresh water. Folklore suggests urinating or dabbing vinegar over the sting, but this doesn't always help. It probably depends on the species of jellyfish that has stung you. Seek medical advice if there are muscle spasms, breathing problems, the sting covers a large area, or is in your eye, ear, or mouth.

Crafting with Shells

On returning home with your collection of shells, wash them well to remove any sand, pat them dry with some paper towel, and then place the shells on some newspaper on a sunny windowsill to dry. Coat the shells with some clear varnish if you want to make them sparkle. You can use shells to decorate greetings cards, matchboxes, jewelry boxes, and pen pots. Or, if you are very creative, you can also try making pieces of jewelry with them. For example, you could wrap some colorful craft cord around a pretty shell and then tie the cord securely to make a simple necklace or bracelet—this is something you could do while still at the beach. If you are lucky enough to find any small shells with predator-bored holes, you can thread seaweed, such as bootlace or dead man's rope (*Chorda filum*), craft cord, or shirring elastic through the hole, and then secure the ends to make a necklace.

MOLLUSKS FOR YOUR SUPPER?

Lots of people enjoy eating mollusks and they provide food for many sea animals too. You can pick your own cockles (clams), razor clams, and mussels from clean beaches, but check the pollution levels of your foraging beach online beforehand. You should cook them as soon as possible when you get home and only eat cooked mollusks from open shells—if a shell doesn't open, throw it away.

Toxic Mollusk Alert

If you are foraging at the beach for mollusks to eat, it's important to watch out for toxic shellfish. Check the sanitary quality of tidal waters with state and environmental agencies before foraging shellfish to eat. Always make sure that the shells of mollusks are completely closed before you cook them. Do not try to force open any shells that fail to open during cooking.

Low tide is the time to rake across the sand if you want to look at clams (*Mercenaria mercenaria*) carefully. You can use a sandbox rake or your hands to scrape through the sand until you feel a hard clam shell. This is the thrill of the beach hunter-gatherer—you can be hands-on. Pop larger clams in a bucket and cook them later if you wish, but always put smaller shells back in the sand. There are more than 500 species of bivalve mollusks on the west coast of North America, including one called a purple clam. You may not see a purple cow, as described in the nonsense verse by Frank Gelett Burgess—"*I never saw a Purple Cow, I never hope to see one, But I can tell you, anyhow, I'd rather see than be one!*"—but you can certainly hunt for a purple clam.

Razor clams leave tiny keyholes on the surface of the sand and at low tide you will sometimes see tremendous squirts of water coming up from the sand and spraying high into the air. You may get wet. Razor clams have a powerful foot which they tighten and relax to burrow in the sand. If you like eating shellfish, the foot is the tastiest

part of the razor clam. If you sprinkle some salt on the keyhole, which razor clams leave in the sand (or where you see a spurt of water), and wait several minutes, a razor clam may be tempted to the surface. In Scotland, razor clams are called spoots because of the water they spray up as they burrow. Foragers of razor clams must grasp the shell swiftly and tightly to win their supper. The shell is sharp; remember that in days gone by, barbers used razor shells to shave gentlemen.

Entice razor clams to the surface with salt.

Use your phone apps for identification.

What Else Can You Spot?

Here is a short beachcomber's list. There are lots of small creatures to spot in the sand and you may like to note down the seabirds and coastal plants and flowers you see too.

Goose barnacles For a long time, barnacles were classified as mollusks because of their shell, but 19th-century scientists decided that they are, in fact, crustaceans. Barnacles are loosely grouped as goose barnacles and acorn barnacles. Goose barnacles are sometimes called gooseneck barnacles because they use a stalk to attach themselves permanently to driftwood or shipwrecks. They are rather strange-looking, but Charles Darwin (see pages 9–10) thought that barnacles were very interesting and spent eight years studying barnacles. This work helped him develop his theory of evolution.

Beach hoppers are easy to identify because they hop. You can often spy them burrowed under seaweed trying to keep cool. Beach hoppers are crustaceans and look like a flattened shrimp. They are sometimes unkindly called sand fleas, but they won't hurt you.

Blood worms leave tiny holes in the sand, which you can see at low tide. They burrow into the sand but only go down so far because there is not enough oxygen in wet sand for them to live.

Whelk egg cases are soft, yellow egg cases that look like bubble wrap. If the case is gray, the whelks have already hatched out, but, if it still yellow, then there may be whelks inside. Baby whelks aren't very kind to their brothers and sisters—the first whelks to hatch will eat their siblings. This means that the whelk is a carnivore. Like conch shells, whelks were used as a musical instrument at the start of a ceremony in some cultures. Whelk egg cases are sometimes called mermaid's necklaces, because the eggs look like a necklace, or fisherman's soap, since the eggs produce a bubbly lather when rubbed in water. Purple whelks were used to make a purple dye by ancient civilizations (see page 64) and Native American tribes.

Sanderlings (*Calidris alba*) are small, pale gray wading birds with long legs that live on sandy beaches. I call them groupies because they meet up and rush about energetically at the point where the sea breaks on to the sand. When one flies off, the rest quickly follow.

Seagrass Not to be confused with the seaweed called sea grass, seagrass (or eelgrass) is a plant that can be found growing in shallow intertidal and subtidal coastal waters (see page 21).

Mollusk Wind Chime

A wind chime made from attractive mollusk shells will remind you of the seashore as it dances noisily in the breeze. When you visit the beach, search for shells that have a natural hole. Empty limpet shells, for example, may already have a neat, circular hole in the middle—made by the limpet's predator—which means you can just thread the craft cord through the hole. Bivalve twin mollusks, such as mussels, cockles, and razor clams, are useful if the two halves of the shell are still attached to each other, because the cord for hanging each shell can be twisted and secured at the shell's natural hinge. This means that you don't have to tie a knot—how shell-crafty is this? (Some coastal areas are treeless, which is why a clothes hanger has been used here, but you could also attach the shells to a stick and suspend your chime with some string.)

WHAT TO USE

- ✔ 12 empty mollusk shells (such as limpets and bivalve mussels, cockles, or razor clams)
- ✔ Bowl of warm, soapy water
- ✔ Spray craft varnish (optional)
- ✔ 12 lengths of colored craft cord, 10–12in (25–30cm) in length
- ✔ Colored plastic clothes hanger
- ✔ Large piece of dulse (*Palmaria palmata*) (optional)

WHAT TO DO

1   Wash your selection of mollusk shells in a bowl of warm, soapy water and dry them carefully.

2   Spray the shells with craft varnish if you want glitzy shells, and leave to dry.

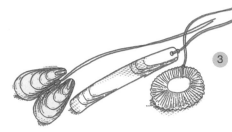

3   Attach each shell to a length of craft cord by threading the cord though the natural hole and tying a knot at one end. You can also just tie the cord around the shell, but this won't be as secure. If you're lucky enough to have joined bivalve shells, simply twist the cord around the hinge.

4 Arrange the threaded shells attractively and then tie the other end of each cord securely around the lower bar of the clothes hanger. Make sure you space the cords so the shells will bounce into each other in the breeze. Attach a large piece of dulse for added color if you wish. The color of the seaweed will fade over time.

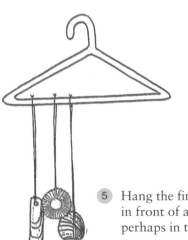

5 Hang the finished wind chime in front of an open window or perhaps in the garden.

Variation

SEAWEED AND SHELL WIND CHIME

When you're at the beach, look for a pretty shell attached to a piece of seaweed (often a member of the wrack family), because this will be perfect for your chime. Simply tie some craft cord to the top of the dried seaweed and then shorten the cord to keep the dangling shells to the same length.

Beach Fun

Sandy beaches at low tide are perfect for beach games. Shingle and pebble beaches are more difficult places for sea life to survive and beach games aren't easy here either. There are, however, lots of plants growing above the high water mark to check out. Low tide is also the best time for a naturalist explorer to visit the seashore and spy on plants and animals that like living underwater.

Play Beach Hopscotch

Hopscotch is a fun hopping game that you can easily play at the beach. Try to finish your game before the tide comes in again and washes away the grid in the sand.

WHAT TO FIND

- ✔ A sandy beach
- ✔ Seaweeds, shells, and flotsam, for naming the grid squares (optional)
- ✔ A marker pebble

THE HOPSCOTCH RULES ARE:

- ✔ You can only put one foot in each square.
- ✔ You have to hop over the square onto which the marker pebble has been thrown.
- ✔ You have to balance on one foot when the pebble has been thrown onto one of the double squares—this is the difficult bit.

WHAT TO DO

1. Draw a hopscotch grid in the sand, as shown here. You can make a longer or shorter grid, if you wish. The design doesn't really matter, but each square needs to be large enough for you to fit one foot in.

2. Use the seaweeds, shells, and flotsam that you've collected to name each square. If you are in a hurry, then just use a pebble to mark traditional numbers in the squares.

3. The idea of the game is to hop on one foot in a single square and with both feet in a double square. The first player throws a marker pebble into the first square and then hops over this square and through the hopscotch grid. If the player gets through, they turn round and hop back through the grid to the start. The player then throws their pebble onto the second square, and so on. If the player lands on a line or tumbles out of the grid, their turn ends.

CREATE BEACH ART

Collect some shells, pebbles, kelp stipes, and flotsam, and arrange them in shapes (e.g. a heart, star, or flower) or perhaps shape the shells and pebbles into a message. Use your imagination in your art and beach games. For example, a length of seaweed can double up as an excellent skipping rope—look out for a thin seaweed called bootlace, mermaid tresses, or dead man's rope (*Chorda filum*). This seaweed lends itself to skipping games. You may find one lengthy enough for long rope games.

You can build sculptures by carefully piling things on top of each other. If you have some string in your knapsack, you can use this to make your creation stable. Sadly, more and more trash is being washed up on beaches, but you can put jetsam to good use in your beach art. Make sure that you take trash home with you when you have finished your beach art and dispose of it properly. We need to keep our beaches clean and tidy—like our bedrooms.

Leave seaweed on the beach, but take plastic man-made "treasure" home with you.

Skipping with sea spaghetti.

Always Be Nature-aware

If you learn as much as you can about the natural world by visiting a local library or researching on a computer, then you'll find the time you spend outdoors even more rewarding. For instance, by reading about and watching crabs you will understand why they molt or cast their outer shells. Similarly, spider crabs are very clever at hiding in seaweed, so if you paddle in rock pools and are patient, sooner or later you will spy these masters of camouflage. A good knowledge of the seashore will help you to respect ocean life. Female horseshoe crabs, for example, struggle ashore to lay their eggs and can lay up to 20 clutches of several thousand eggs, which are the size of caviar. Only a few will hatch. A kind person, however, might wrongly think that the crab should be returned to the sea. This would be such a waste of the horseshoe crab's effort and is a good example of why we need to learn how the natural world works.

Check Tide Times

Before you visit the beach, it's important to check the tide times. Remember that, although a low spring tide reveals sea life, a high spring tide means that there will only be a mini beach for you to play on.

4

Water and Wetlands

When it is snowing have you ever thrown back your head, opened your mouth wide, and eaten snow? Water comes in many guises, including rain, mist, hail, and snow. Fresh water is found in rivers, streams, ponds, lakes, and canals, but excludes seawater and brackish waters (which are saline but not as salty as seawater). You can have lots of fun by wild water, making mud pies, sailing toy rafts, and skimming stones, or you can simply be still and listen as the wind blows through the reeds and willows.

Wild Water

Wild water isn't always the same: sometimes it's murky and calm; at other times, fast-flowing and clear. The water in a lake or pond doesn't flow anywhere—it is still. This is known as a lentic ecosystem. You can remember this by the letter "e" in lentic and the word end—the water ends (or remains) in the lake or pond. Flowing water is called a lotic ecosystem—remember the letter "o" in onward, which is exactly what flowing water does: it flows onward.

WATERY WORLDS IN MINIATURE

As well as the speed of the water's flow and its salinity, the depth of the water is also important. Combined, they determine the plant and animal life that will flourish in or near ponds and rivers. You can explore the miniature inhabitants that live in wild water by collecting a sample from a murky, lowland pond in a glass jar and studying it under a magnifying glass—you will see lots of tiny organisms. Compare this sample with water collected in a jar from a high, sparkling mountain stream. Under a microscope you won't see much wildlife in the clearer water. You may, however, want to cup your hands and splash the clean mountain water over your face. You wouldn't want to do this with cloudy, green pond water. When you swim or wade out to the deeper parts of a lake, you can feel the temperature of the water change; this is known as the thermocline—where cool waters meet sun-heated surface water. *Thermo* comes from the Greek word for "hot" and *clino* from the word for "slope." The temperature of the water also influences plant and animal life. Light is important as well, since the sun provides plants with the energy to manufacture their own food through a process called photosynthesis (see page 37).

Be a Pollution Detective

Collect water from a pond or river in a jar and become a pollution detective. The presence or absence of plant and animal life can act as a guide to levels of pollution.

✱ If the water is clean you may see mayflies and stoneflies. They're the first to buzz off if water is polluted. Trout and minnow only live in clean water too. The diversity of plants and invertebrates is also a clue to the health of the water.

✱ Natural waste from living and dead freshwater organisms is "recycled" by tiny organisms called bacteria—it's humans who cause pollution. If you see dumped rubbish in a pond or river, tell your local environmental agency and offer to help with organized pond and river conservation.

Go Pond Dipping

Morning and early afternoon are the best times for pond dipping because small creatures respond to the sun's warmth and there is plenty of light for you to study them. Most wildlife lives among the plants at the edges of rivers and ponds, rather than in open water, so this is the best (and easiest) place to start dipping. The equipment you'll need is inexpensive, but you might like to make your own pond dipping net (see page 114). Here are some helpful tips for pond dipping:

❋ Vary your dipping area. Remember that plants and animals differ according to habitat. Some are found in deep water, others near the surface.

❋ Tread slowly and quietly as you near the water so that your reflection and vibrations from your footsteps do not frighten away tadpoles, beetles, and small fish from the shallow water. Think like a predator.

❋ Take jars, lids with air holes, and white food trays with you for collecting bugs. Plastic bottles and buckets are especially useful because they won't break. (A large plastic bottle with the narrow top cut off makes a cheap bucket.)

❋ A kitchen sieve is helpful for looking through fine gravel and mud. You'll find a pair of tweezers, a white plastic spoon, and a small paintbrush useful too, so remember to pop these in your wild knapsack (see page 8). A white (to help visibility) ice cube tray also has lots of compartments for viewing tiny bugs.

❋ Keep a pocket magnifying glass, notebook, and pencil close at hand.

❋ Sweep your net quickly in a figure-of-eight pattern and tip the contents into your jar, tray, or bucket as soon as you can.

❋ Look among the leaves and twigs at the bottom of the pond with your dipping net.

❋ Sift through water plants and grasses trailing in water. Use your paintbrush or white plastic spoon to gently flick insects into jars.

❋ In fast-flowing streams, look under large stones or on the bank sides.

❋ Transfer the bugs to a jar or white food tray half-filled with pond water. The white background of the tray will make it easier to study the bugs with a magnifying glass.

❋ Jot down plants and animals as you spot them in your notepad, because your memory is never as good as the wild experience. Keep a dated pond diary if you visit regularly.

❋ Pond wildlife is small and delicate, and can be easily harmed. All creatures and plant material should be returned to the pond once you've looked at them.

Keep Safe by Water

Young children in particular should *always* have adult supervision when exploring and having fun by water.

Collect pond water and sludge to study.

Trees that Like Damp Soil

Trees need different soil conditions to thrive. Sun-loving olive trees, for example, don't need a lot of water. Aspens like sunshine too, but prefer moist soil. Here are some species that have adapted well to boggy and damp land.

THE GUELDER ROSE (*Viburnum opulus*) This plant belongs to the same family as the elder and was once called swamp elder because it likes boggy land. It has brilliant, shiny, scarlet berries, which are popular with bullfinches. The berries hang on the tree until winter. You can collect the berries and stick them to a *Bird-feeding Roll* (see pages 132–33).

THE ALDER (*Alnus glutinosa*) Alders grow in the wet soil by streams and in wetlands. When young, their leaves feel sticky and stretchy. The caterpillar-like catkins appear in spring before the leaves. The catkins are beautiful—they have tints of mauve and red, as well as green. The pollinated female catkins become woody and look like Lilliputian fruits, but are, in fact, cones. They open up to release seeds, which are dispersed by wind and water. Collect the cones for use in craftwork or pop them in a mini nature treasure box.

Willow tree

THE WEEPING WILLOW (*Salix babylonica* and hybrids) Like the alder, the weeping willow has splendid spring catkins (flowers). The catkins are a favorite with early spring bees, which buzz in to gather nectar and pollen. The male catkins are yellow and the females green. The willow is a useful tree because its tangled roots bind the soil and stop riverbanks from slipping into the river. Marram grass (*Ammophila arenaria*) does much the same job in sand dunes. Sprays of pussy willow (*Salix* spp.) are often used as palms in churches on Palm Sunday (which is the Sunday before Easter). Clever crafts people use willow branches for weaving into furniture and in coffins for "green" burials. Marram grass is good for weaving too. Native Americans were fans of the willow tree's pain-relieving properties—willow bark contains a substance called salicin, which works like aspirin.

Alder cones

Making Artist's Charcoal from Pussy Willow

If you are a budding naturalist artist, you might like to try using willow twigs to produce charcoal. Charcoal is easy to make—you've probably seen charcoaled sticks in the embers of a bonfire. Try to avoid using young or treated wood. This is because young wood produces soft, powdery charcoal and treated wood may give off toxic fumes. Also shun very thin twigs because the wood will shrink as it turns to charcoal and the charcoal will be too thin to draw with. You'll need to make sure that the twigs you use are dry too. Harder woods take longer to turn to charcoal, with the exact charring time depending on the thickness of the sticks and the number of twigs wrapped in the package, so have lots of fun experimenting. As with everything, practice makes perfect.

WHAT TO USE

- ✔ Penknife
- ✔ 6 twigs of dry, soft wood (such as willow or pine), 6in (15cm) in length and no thicker than your thumb
- ✔ 5 squares of kitchen foil, 14 x 14in (35 x 35cm)
- ✔ Barbecue
- ✔ Pair of tongs

WHAT TO DO

1. Use the penknife to remove any joints in the twigs so that they are as straight as possible. This will make it easier to hold them.

2. Carefully scrape the bark from the twigs with the penknife.

3. Lay the twigs on a square of foil and wrap this tightly around them to make a parcel. Make sure there isn't any air in the package, because air will encourage ash and not charcoal. Continue to wrap with the remaining sheets of foil.

4. Place the package on the grid of a barbecue and when the flames have died down—or once you've finished cooking your sausages—use a pair of tongs to push the package into the center of the hot coals. Pile the coals around the package and leave overnight.

5. In the morning, when the package is completely cold, unwrap your charcoal and start drawing.

Variations

BONFIRE AND OVEN CHARCOAL

If you are having a bonfire, try putting the end of a stick into the embers of the dying fire and leave it to blacken for 10 minutes. Carefully remove the stick, allow it to cool, and then use the blackened end to write with—a natural pencil. You can also make charcoal in the oven of a range cooker. Pop the foil-wrapped package in a hot oven and char for 12–15 hours, depending on the thickness of the sticks.

The Wind in the Willows

You might like to read Kenneth Grahame's book *The Wind in the Willows*. First published in 1908, it is a magical tale of the riverside wildlife characters of Ratty, Mole, Toad, and Badger. Many of Ratty and Mole's adventures take place by the river and the elegant weeping willow features in their travels.

Make a Pond Dipping Net

You can use a net for dipping in ponds and rivers, or in rock pools at the beach. Nets made from natural wood are the best because they don't rust, which can weaken the net at the top. If you are clever, you may find a stick that is pitched like a hayfork (a pitched fork), which you can just slip the net over. This means that you won't have to create a circle of bendy wood. The stick needs to be the right size for the person who is dipping, so hunt carefully for a stick that nature has made to measure for you.

WHAT TO USE

- ✔ An old pair of pantyhose (tights)
- ✔ Scissors
- ✔ Needle and thread
- ✔ A bendy stick (such as willow) or a stick that forks
- ✔ Strong string or plastic-coated wire

WHAT TO DO

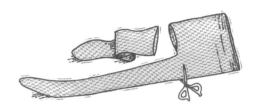

1. Cut off the legs from the pair of pantyhose (tights) using the scissors.

2. Sew up the leg holes using the needle and thread to make your homemade net.

3. Bend the stick to form a loop that you can push your net over. Keep the loop in place by using the string or plastic-coated wire to attach it to the handle of the stick. An extra pair of hands may be needed here to hold the loop steady as you fix it in place.

4. Slip the net over the loop or pitched stick (the elastic around the top of the pantyhose will keep it in position) and you have a dipping net.

Net Construction Tips

✳ The dipping net must be strong enough not to bend when you sweep it quickly through water or water plants.

✳ If you can't find a long, bendy stick, then make a loop from a wire clothes hanger and attach this to the end of a long, straight stick before slipping over the net.

✳ Nylon, or a material with a thin mesh, allows water to pass through quickly. Heavier materials such as cotton won't work because water passes through much too slowly and so your pond dipping won't be such fun.

Aquatic Plants

Aquatic plants like to grow in or by the edges of rivers and ponds. Green underwater plants often resemble a tropical rainforest, while marsh marigolds (*Caltha palustris*) and water lilies can be colorful.

WONDERFUL WATER LILIES (*Nymphaea* **spp.**) There are over 60 varieties of water lily worldwide, and some are very exotic. The Ancient Egyptians even worshipped a water lily called the sacred lotus. White water lilies may look out of place in wild Scottish lochans (or small lakes) or in muddy streams but they are, in fact, a wild flower. The pads of the lilies float like rafts; some leaves are big enough to seat a large group of water-nymph stick people. Smaller leaves may be heart-shaped and provide a perfect float for a more delicate stick fairy. (Turn to page 52 to learn how to make *Fun Flower and Stick People*.) The stems and leaves of water lilies were once considered a delicacy and still are in some countries. Amphibians (i.e. animals that divide their time between water and land) also like eating lily leaves.

During the day the flowers of water lilies float on the surface of the water and, as the sun fades, they close tightly. The water lily pulls in its petals just like a shopkeeper pulls down the shutters of a store at the end of the working day. If, however, you watch a water lily carefully on a dull day, the flower may not bother to open at all. Shopkeepers have to open whatever the weather; water lily flowers are fair-weather flora.

Water lilies are anchored deep under water by firm rhizomes (which are swollen underground stems). In winter the flowers die back and are nourished by food stored in the rhizomes. New stems pop up in the spring. Water lilies are pollinated by insects and, when the lily fruit is ripe, it sinks to the river bed and the seeds pop out and float away to waters new.

Try sketching water lilies with some homemade charcoal (see page 113). If you're interested in capturing finer details, then draw the insects napping on water lily pads. If you sit quietly by a pond you may hear frogs croaking too.

DUCKWEED (*Lemna* **spp.**) Some water plants such as common or lesser duckweed (*Lemna minor*) float at the water's surface. Duckweed is also called duck meat—I'll leave you to work out why. It is one of the smallest pond plants and grows in shallow water because it needs lots of light. Duckweed provides shelter for wildlife and food for many organisms.

Duckweed leaves each produce a new plant—try putting some duckweed in a jar and seeing if it multiplies. A new leaf will grow from a slit in an old leaf. If you like watching pond wildlife, pop some duckweed in a fish tank filled with water to make a plant aquarium. Keep any duckweed under control because otherwise it will stop the plants below getting any light. This is important because plants need light to photosynthesize in order to make food and produce oxygen. If you put a jar of pond weed in sunshine, you should see bubbles of oxygen. In 1774, a clergyman called Dr Joseph Priestley discovered oxygen while experimenting in a pond in Calne, Wiltshire, England.

Flowers, Herbs, and Grasses

Meadowsweet

Every wetland plant has adapted to wet growing conditions. Some wetland plants such as meadowsweet are scented, while others like watercress and water mint are helpful to a wild cook.

MEADOWSWEET (*Filipendula ulmaria*) grows on the banks of streams and ditches. In midsummer, as the blossom on the elder tree fades, meadowsweet raises its blousy cream head. After dusk its honey scent fills the air— perhaps this is why the Druids considered it to be a sacred herb. In Medieval times it was used as a strewing herb to make rooms smell nice. It is sometimes referred to as Queen of the Meadow and was a favorite of Queen Elizabeth I (1533–1603). Country people suggest that its scent helps cure a headache and, indeed, salicylic acid was isolated from meadowsweet to make the headache pill aspirin. The red stems of meadowsweet are brittle and the underside of its three-pronged leaves downy. Use the blossom in your wild kitchen in any recipe that calls for elderflowers (see *Meadowsweet Diluting Syrup*, on pages 152–53). Nature is clever: meadowsweet begins to flower when the elderflower is over.

WATERCRESS (*Rorippa nasturtium-aquaticum*) Plants come and go with the seasons, but watercress has a spring and second fall (autumn) growth. Watercress grows by streams and tastes the same as the watercress you can buy in stores. It belongs to the cabbage family and is a useful ingredient in the wild kitchen. The older stems are the tastiest.

Watercress Warning

Beware of picking and eating watercress from streams where cattle and sheep loiter because it can make you sick. This is due to the presence of a flat worm called liver fluke (*Fasciola hepatica*). The worm attacks the liver of cattle and sheep, and can kill humans too. The worm's larva begins its life in sheep or cow droppings. The mobile larva hatches in damp conditions and then heads off for water, where a gastropod mud snail called *Galba truncatula* lives. The larva burrows into the soft tissue of the snail and eventually metamorphoses (transforms) into an adult liver fluke. The adult fluke then swims off to hide among plants like watercress, waiting for grazing animals or foraging humans to restart the life cycle. This sounds nasty but if you cook the watercress properly, you will also kill the liver fluke. That said: it's safer to pick wild watercress where it is growing in fast-flowing streams, far away from grazing animals.

Grazing animals ingest the liver fluke and the life cycle begins again.

Liver fluke eggs are shed 8–12 weeks after the animal is infected.

Adult liver flukes look for a final host (e.g. grazing animals such cows and sheep).

Liver fluke larvae search for an intermediate host (usually a snail).

Gastropod mud snail

WILD WATER MINT (*Mentha aquatica*) is another useful plant for your wild kitchen. You can use this herb instead of pineapple weed in a wild teabag (see *Pineapple Weed Tea*, on page 151). In common with other wild herbs, its flavor isn't as strong as the garden variety. You'll need to use more, not less, wild mint to make your food or drink taste minty.

WILD THYME (*Thymus polytrichus*) Although I've included wild thyme in this chapter, you will find it growing in a variety of places: on rocky coasts, downland, and grassland, but also in boggy ground. Wild flora and fauna don't always fit into just one book chapter. The best time to pick wild herbs is in the morning when the dew has gone, but before the sun becomes hot. If you rub wild *thyme* on your hands they will smell nice, but it won't leave you with *time* on your hands… that is a very bad joke. You might enjoy running barefoot on wild thyme and treating your feet to some free aromatherapy, but you'll have to move buzzing bees and butterflies on their way first. On sunny days, butterflies and bees feast on the nectar of wild thyme and they like wild mint too. Wild thyme can be tied in a bunch with other herbs and added to casseroles, or the leaves can be stripped and popped in muslin to make a teabag. You can add wild thyme to baking recipes too.

Wild thyme

Mixed herbs

YELLOW IRIS (*Iris pseudacorus*) or yellow flag grows in marshy or swampy areas. It's a sturdy plant and Hebridean children use the stems as swords in mock battles. It has a cheerful yellow flower in late spring and its broad flat leaves are useful for craftwork. For example, you could use them to weave a sail for a toy raft or to make some natural place mats (see *Make Your Own Toy Raft*, on pages 125–27).

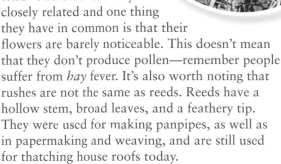

Yellow iris

RUSHES, GRASSES, AND SEDGES are very closely related and one thing they have in common is that their flowers are barely noticeable. This doesn't mean that they don't produce pollen—remember people suffer from *hay* fever. It's also worth noting that rushes are not the same as reeds. Reeds have a hollow stem, broad leaves, and a feathery tip. They were used for making panpipes, as well as in papermaking and weaving, and are still used for thatching house roofs today.

Most people have sat on a chair made from bamboo, which is a type of grass. In the *Adventures of Huckleberry Finn* (published in 1885), an adventure story by Mark Twain, the cane with which Aunt Polly tries to beat Huckleberry's friend, Tom Sawyer, may well have been *Arundinaria gigantea*—this is the only bamboo that is native to the United States. Sedges often grow by the seashore, in marshes, or on riverbanks. They like damp and boggy ground. Common cotton grass (*Eriophorum angustifolium*) is a funny-looking plant and, in spite of its name, is a *sedge* and not a grass. Its seedhead looks and feels like cotton wool and provides food for caterpillars and black grouse. There is species of cotton grass called hare's tail cotton grass (*Eriophorum vaginatum*), which has a single ball of fluff that resembles

If you go loch-dipping, look out for aquatic plants as well as small creatures.

Grasses and rushes

a hare's tail. The downy cotton heads were once used to stuff pillows. If you make doll house bedding or pincushions for a sewing box, you can use cotton grass seedheads as stuffing. When some of the pond sedges are in flower, the seedy heads look as if they could be used to chant the *False Oats Rhyme* (see page 53), but don't try with this one or you may suffer a sharp grass cut. It is easy to cut yourself on grass. While you are gathering cotton grass, look carefully and you may be lucky and find some cranberries growing nearby.

WILD CRANBERRIES (*Vaccinium macrocarpon*) like boggy ground and were a favorite of Native Americans who called them *sassamanash*. In spring, the small cranberry flowers are bright pink. You may spot the flowers, but this doesn't always guarantee fruit. The fall (autumn) cranberry fruit grows close to the ground and turns from pink to red as it ripens. It is a rather podgy

Common cotton grass

fruit for such a tiny stem. Wild cranberries taste sour and are really useful in the kitchen—they will keep for over a month if stored in a cool place and can be frozen too. Remember that cranberries grow close to the ground, which will be boggy or very wet, so forage on your bare knees or wear some waterproofs.

BISTORT (*Persicaria amphibia*) In a bog or floating on water you may see a pink-headed flower called bistort. This is an aquatic version of the land-based bistort *Persicaria bistorta*. Bistort takes its name from Medieval Latin and means "twice-twisted," because its root is very twisted. The cooked leaves were once used in a savory "cleansing" pudding called Passion Dock, which was made in Lent (the 40 days before Easter). You can cook bistort leaves in your wild kitchen, but you may find them a little bitter. The pretty pink flowers, when dried and pressed, look attractive on homemade cards (see *Press Wild Flowers and Grasses*, on page 55).

LADY'S SMOCK (*Cardamine pratensis*) In spring look out for another pink flower called lady's smock. It is sometimes called cuckooflower. This plant likes damp places and is called the cuckooflower because it blooms when the cuckoo arrives in the United Kingdom. The flowers are a food source for butterflies and other insects, but the bitter leaves can be picked when young and used in salads.

Some Water and Wetland Wildlife

Wetlands are wonderful places for watching and studying wildlife because all life-forms need water. When visiting a pond or wetland area, see how many different insects, amphibians, or water-loving mammals you can spot.

FRESHWATER SNAILS

Most mollusks live in the sea, the gastropod being the only type of mollusk to have moved inland from the coast. Freshwater snails live in rivers, lakes, and ponds, while the garden snail lives on land. You can usually find a terrestrial (land) snail guzzling on leaves in a vegetable garden. The shell of a baby snail is called a protoconch (original shell). It is very soft, but hardens as it grows. The shell grows with the snail and the original baby shell ends up in the center of the spiral. As the snail grows, new whorls are added inside the shell. The number of rings (whorls) gives an approximate age for the snail, in much the same way that counting the rings on a tree stump tells you the age of the tree. Great pond snails usually curl to the right, but you could look for a left-hander. The snail comes out of its mobile home to feed and most snails have an operculum (a watertight trap door), which is protective and prevents land snails from drying out.

Water snails are tough. They can handle low or warm temperatures, foul water, and even survive without water for a period of time. They are divided into two groups depending on how they breathe: the pulmonates float up to the surface to take a gulp of air into a lung-like cavity, while the prosobranchs use gills to absorb oxygen from the water.

Freshwater snail

DRAGONFLIES AND DAMSELFLIES

These sun-worshipping insects belong to the order known as Odonata, which comes from the Greek word for "tooth." This is because they have toothed jaws. On sunny days, when there is little wind, damselflies and dragonflies can often be seen skimming over ponds, as they hover and catch insects with their feet. There are lots of species (kinds) of dragonflies and damselflies and their color changes as they grow up. Adult frogs like eating damselflies and dragonflies, so they're on the look out for them too.

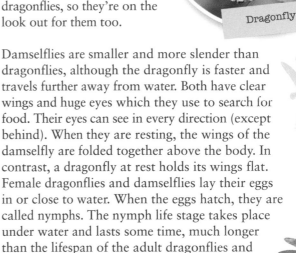

Dragonfly

Damselflies are smaller and more slender than dragonflies, although the dragonfly is faster and travels further away from water. Both have clear wings and huge eyes which they use to search for food. Their eyes can see in every direction (except behind). When they are resting, the wings of the damselfly are folded together above the body. In contrast, a dragonfly at rest holds its wings flat. Female dragonflies and damselflies lay their eggs in or close to water. When the eggs hatch, they are called nymphs. The nymph life stage takes place under water and lasts some time, much longer than the lifespan of the adult dragonflies and damselflies. As the nymph grows, it sheds its skin; this is called molting. Sadly, the adult life of a damselfly can be measured in weeks, not months.

AMPHIBIANS

Amphibians such as frogs and toads live on the land and in the water. Frogs live on land, close to water, because they need to keep their skin moist. They spend more time in water than toads, which live in drier places. Frogs begin life as an egg in water. Frogspawn is laid in early spring. The female frog lays thousands of eggs to ensure that some survive, because many will be eaten by fish, newts, and beetles. The egg hatches into a tadpole, which has a head, body, and tail. The tadpole grows four legs and metamorphoses into a frog. Lots of frogs spawn in garden ponds, so you may have frogs in your own backyard. If you look carefully, you may even find frogspawn in a watering can or puddle. Older people used to put frogspawn in glass jars, and watch it turn into tadpoles at home or in school. Today naturalists think that it's kinder to spy on frogspawn and tadpoles in the wild.

WATER-LOVING MAMMALS

Some mammals, especially beavers and otters, live mainly in the water. If you are very lucky, you may even spot a water vole on a sunny day as it searches for food, although sadly these are now on the Red Data List of endangered species.

BEAVERS These mammals are clever because they build dams in streams and so create pools. Wildlife and humans need water and so beavers help humans by slowing down the journey of a stream from its source to the sea, holding it up behind dams and spreading it sideways into the land as bogs, pools, and riffles (shallow or rocky parts of a stream where the water flows more slowly), where so much life can flourish.

Beavers also cut down trees at the water's edge, so allowing more sunlight to reach the water and riverbank and helping flowers to grow. Beaver-felled tree trunks create homes for lichen, fungi, and insects, which then provide food for birds and mammals. Trees felled by beavers also provide perches and nesting places for birds, while their leaves can be reached by browsing deer. Woodpeckers and owls sometimes make their homes in holes in dead trees, where they then have access to ready-made food.

Beavers dig burrows and build homes called lodges at the water's edge. When baby beavers (called kits) are still living in the lodge, their parents teach them to swim in a sort of indoor swimming pool. They grow up to be very good swimmers and can hold their breath underwater for up to 20 minutes.

Make a Waterside Den

If you enjoy studying frogs, make a special den near a pond that has frogspawn and pop back regularly to check up on the developing tadpoles. You could sweep out the den, float a toy raft on the water, or do some weaving (see page 126). You could also leave a tracking tunnel. Cut the ends off a plastic bottle and cover it with black plastic. Pop a piece of white tissue paper and a blob of peanut butter inside the bottle. Place the tunnel in a muddy area—when you return, the bait should have gone and you can study the muddy footprints with your magnifying glass.

OTTERS The largest member of the weasel family, otters like swimming in beaver-built pools as they hunt for fish. Otters are good at diving and holding their breath under water too. Juvenile otters, which are called pups, become great fish-catching divers before they leave their mothers at the age of about six months.

SOME FLYING POND DIPPERS

Also look out for ducks—the green-headed mallard (*Anas platyrhynchos*) is the most common—and smaller black moorhens. The colorful kingfisher may stop by to do a spot of fishing if you are extremely quiet and lucky. With more luck on your side, an early bird may pull back the curtains and spy a heron visiting their garden stream or pond. Interestingly, this bird nests colonially in woods, not wetlands.

Beaver

Common Pond Wildlife

There may be a thousand or more different species living in a small pond or stretch of river, from tiny microscopic creatures to cold-blooded (reptiles) and warm-blooded (mammals) animals. Wetlands act as an ecosystem. Each life form living here helps the other creatures to survive in some way. Think of it as a closely connected water-loving community.

Dragonfly

Heron

Kingfisher

Otter

Water vole

Leaping salmon

Mayfly

Tracking Wildlife

Getting close to wildlife is something you can do with family or friends, or with an organized group. You could join a local bird-watching club and quietly observe birds from a hide with an experienced teacher. Whatever route you take, you will become closer to nature. Watching wild animals is, however, a difficult activity because they can sense danger and their hearing is much better than ours. Wildlife will sense a human a long time before we see or hear them. This is why tracking is such a good way of spying on animals.

WHAT IS TRACKING?

Tracking is an ancient art that prehistoric hunter-gatherers relied upon to survive. You can buy food in a store, but learning hunter-gatherer naturalist skills will help connect you with nature, as well as appreciate how interdependent we are with the natural world. You will better understand why we must protect rare species and care for the environment.

Scientists track animals to work out why certain populations are shrinking. They tag animals and use transmitters to track migration patterns. Tracking also helps conservationists. When you hear the phrase: "Here come the vultures," you may think of somebody swooping in to finish off a cake. When we say, "The vultures are circling," it's actually a signal that somebody is in danger of failing. Scientists at Columbia University, in the United States, who fitted GPS transmitters to 39 vultures and tracked them for several months, proved that these everyday vulture sayings are accurate. The vulture tracking study helped conservationists because they learnt that vultures focus on death traps, rather than migrating herds. This easy-prey attitude has led to two species of vulture being placed on the Red Data List of endangered species.

WHERE TO GO TRACKING

Some wild areas and weather conditions are better for tracking wildlife than others. For example, following animal and bird prints in snow is easy because the tracks show up more clearly. If you go into the garden early in the morning, after snow has fallen, you'll be surprised by the number of paw-shaped (animal) and fork-shaped (bird) tracks that have appeared while you've been asleep. A light fall of fresh snow creates the best tracking conditions. Dogs leave pointed tracks, while cats leave rounded paw marks. If deer come into the garden, there may be two-toe-hooved tracks too. In North America there may be antelope or mountain goats. These hoof marks are similar but different to those of deer. Wild boar tracks are hoof-shaped too. Otter tracks have five toes, which arch around the front of a large pad. In soft ground, you may be able to see claw marks and the webs between toes. A good field track and poo (droppings) book or phone app will help you to identify the different tracks you come across.

It's easy to spot bird prints on damp sand, at low tide on the seashore. On dry land, however, tracking isn't as easy. Wetlands are a very good place to track birds and other wildlife because the ground is damp. Bogs are not such a good idea, but anywhere where the ground is wet but firm shows tracks up well.

Bird footprints in sand

Rabbit footprints in snow

Helpful Tracking Tips

Here are some tracking thoughts and questions to ask:

* Where do the tracks stop? If they stop by a tree, is it a squirrel track? (See if you can spot the difference between a squirrel and hedgehog print.)

* How close together are the tracks? Was the animal moving quickly or slowly?

* Look for holes in the ground and at the bottom of trees. Does the hole still house an animal? Have leaves blown into the hole or has there been recent soil disturbance?

* Look for tracks by puddles. Running through a muddy puddle usually leaves a footprint. You can try this out for yourself.

* Stranded seaweed provides food for sand-hoppers, so look for their holes in the sand.

* After you've spotted the tracks, look about for less obvious signs of wildlife presence. Look out for fur on barbed wire, as well as upturned stones and broken twigs.

* For night tracking, it is best to have a green LED tracking flashlight or torch.

* Frogs have small feet with five long toes; the second toe is usually the longest. Frogs jump, so the tracks will be grouped at regular intervals (from jump to jump).

* In snow you can check out the pattern and size of yellow (urine) calling cards left by wildlife.

* Pop a coin by the track or dropping and take a photograph. The coin will give you a sense of its size.

* Wild animals nibble away at fir cones to eat the seeds. Clever trackers can work out which animal has eaten a nut by studying the way the shell was cracked open (see *Who Ate the Nuts, Fungi, and Cones?*, on page 45).

Remember: Leave no tracks in the countryside apart from your own footprints.

HOW TO TRACK

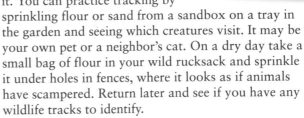

Tracking can be as simple or complicated as you want to make it. You can practice tracking by sprinkling flour or sand from a sandbox on a tray in the garden and seeing which creatures visit. It may be your own pet or a neighbor's cat. On a dry day take a small bag of flour in your wild rucksack and sprinkle it under holes in fences, where it looks as if animals have scampered. Return later and see if you have any wildlife tracks to identify.

You can check out who is eating your garden vegetables by looking for droppings. Rabbits, for example, are plant-eaters and, like other herbivores (plant-eating animals), their droppings are rounded, fibrous, and usually in a pile. Deer pellets are cylindrical and shiny, and found in heaped piles. The droppings from carnivores (meat-eating animals) often contain fur and bone. Some animals leave droppings in a latrine to mark or claim their territory. Badgers place pyramids of musky-scented poo in a latrine, usually close to their sett (where they live). Otter spraints (droppings) are made of fish bones and scales, with other small bones, and perhaps fur or feathers bound together by a black tarry mucous. Fresh spraints are sticky and have a sweet, musky smell. Older droppings harden and become gray and crumbly. Poke at poo (droppings) with a stick or wearing plastic gloves (*not* with your bare hands).

Become a Bone Detective

Animals with backbones are called vertebrates. In mammals, the skeleton is on the inside and acts as a frame on which the body is built. The skeleton grows with the mammal. While you are tracking, look out for bones. Some wildlife is nocturnal and their bones are often the only evidence of their existence. Bone I.D. is challenging, but there is a lot to be learnt from looking at bones. If you find a jaw, for example, the teeth are helpful in species I.D. You can work out if the animal was a herbivore, carnivore, or omnivore (an animal that eats both plants and animals). A herbivore (plant eater) has strong molars for grinding and small or no canine teeth; a carnivore has pointed canine teeth and sharp incisors for eating meat; an omnivore (an animal that eats both plants and animals) has a combination of sharp and grinding teeth. Age can also be determined—look and see if the teeth are worn. If so, the animal was old. Once you get the basics, you're on the road to becoming a bone detective.

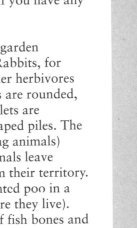

Water Fun

Play Poohstick

You can have great fun by water leaping across stepping stones, making mud pies, or skimming stones. Remember to take a change of clothes with you, though, in case you get wet.

Have fun leaping across stepping stones.

HOP ON STEPPING STONES

Stepping on stones to cross a stream is sensible fun because it means you won't get wet. It's a simple game but you will have to work out the quickest and safest route across the stream, as well as how to shift your balance as you stone hop and jump. If you don't manage to do this, you will get rather damp. As with lots of wild adventures, practice makes perfect.

MAKE MUD PIES

The idea of making a three-tiered cake for a mud pie bake-off came from Anna and Katie Campbell, 14-year-old twins from the Isle of South Uist, off the Scottish mainland. Mud pie creations are fun for all age groups. This activity calls for a follow-up swim in a loch, lake, river, or the sea, or perhaps a hot, soapy bath. The buckets and spades will need a good rinse out too.

Play Poohsticks

Poohsticks first appeared in A.A. Milne's children's story *The House at Pooh Corner* (1928). Pooh accidentally drops a fir cone in the water and discovers that it reappears on the other side of the bridge. Children use sticks instead of fir cones to play the game. You will need at least two players, a person to be the starter, and a safe bridge to play this game. Younger children should have an adult close by when playing near water.

To play, choose a stick each. Check which way the stream is flowing. The players must face the stream on the side where it flows under the bridge (looking upstream). Each player holds his or her stick at arm's length. The starter should make sure the taller children lower their arms so all the sticks start at the same level. The starter then orders: "On your marks, get set, go!" and the sticks are dropped (not thrown) into the running water. The players rush across the bridge to the other side to see which stick comes through first. The winner is the owner of the first stick under the bridge.

Making mud pies is messy.

Skimming Stones

This traditional game is best played on a sunny windless day. The idea is simple: hold a flat stone between your finger and thumb and throw it onto water so it skims the surface as many times as possible before finally sinking. To play, pick a stone that is as thin and light as possible. Throw the stone with as much force as you can, as horizontally as possible, and from as low to the ground as you can bend, while ensuring that you are still able to swing your arm to throw. The key to a good throw is to spin the stone.

Make Your Own Toy Raft

You can have lots of fun sailing a toy raft in streams and ponds. You can build a simple wooden raft or attach a separate mast and sail as well if you wish. You will need to cut some sticks or small branches to make the base of the raft using a pair of hand pruners (secateurs). Turn to pages 126–27 to find out how to make a mast and sail.

Turn to pages 126–27 to find out how to make a mast and sail.

WHAT TO USE

- ✔ 20 thick sticks or small branches (of an even thickness), measuring 9–12in (23–30cm) in length
- ✔ String
- ✔ Scissors
- ✔ Corks (optional)

WHAT TO DO

1. Choose the two thickest sticks to act as support sticks. Take the first of these support sticks and attach a length of string, about ½in (1cm) or so from one end of the stick. Put the other support stick to one side.

2. Tie the first of your remaining sticks to the first support stick. (You don't need to use knots—just wrap the string tightly on both sides of the support stick in a continuous figure-of-eight pattern.)

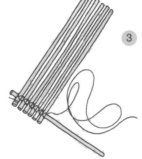

3. Use the string to bind a second stick tightly to the support stick. Continue binding the raft sticks to the support stick until you reach about ½in (1cm) from the other end. Now you need to tie a firm knot around the support stick.

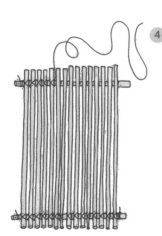

4. With all of the raft sticks attached to the first support stick, you should now have only the second support stick remaining. Take this stick and start tying the other end of all the raft sticks to it in the same way as you did for the first support stick. Keep the string as tight as you can, weaving it in and out of the sticks as you bind them securely to the second support stick. When you have finished, tie a firm knot and cut the string. You now have a simple but useful toy raft.

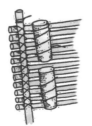

5. If your raft needs help to float, tie some corks to the side or underneath. Tie a long piece of string to make a tether to stop your raft floating away.

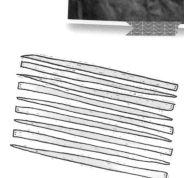

Weaving a sail for your raft

WHAT TO USE

- ✔ Approximately 20 long, flat leaves (*Iris* leaves are ideal)
- ✔ 1–2 extra-large, long leaves, torn into thin strips
- ✔ Strong, thin twine or string (colored if you wish)
- ✔ 3 sticks, 2 a little shorter than the raft sticks and 1 about one and a half times as long as the raft sticks
- ✔ Penknife
- ✔ Table knife or scissors

WHAT TO DO

1 Lay out half (about 9 or 10) of the long leaves, arranging them so that the tip of the first is pointing to the left and the tip of the next one is pointing to the right. Continue alternating the leaves in rows as neatly as you can.

2 Lay out the other half (again about 9 or 10) of the leaves, but this time up and down and not sideways. Again, alternate the tips and stalks as in Step 1.

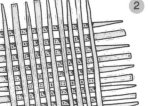

3 The next stage is a little tricky. Take the lowest of your side-to-side leaves and weave it in between the up-and-down leaves (one below, the next above, the next below, and so on until you reach the end). The tips and stalks of every leaf should remain free.

4 Take the next lowest side-to-side leaf and do the same, but this time weave one above first and one below next. (To start with your leaves may slip on each other, but they should begin to hold their shape by the third leaf.)

5 Continue weaving with each leaf in turn in the opposite way to the one before and the one after it.

6 When you have finished, your sail will have untidy edges all the way round. So, carefully fold over each leaf and tuck it into the weaving (i.e. back onto itself).

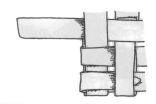

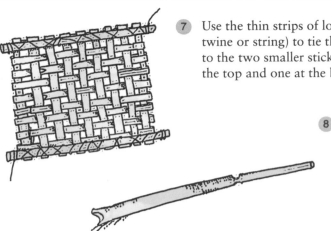

7 Use the thin strips of long leaves (or some twine or string) to tie the nearly square sail to the two smaller sticks, with one stick at the top and one at the bottom.

8 Use the remaining large stick to create the sail's mast. Make a small notch with the penknife in the bottom of the thicker end (this will form the base of the mast) so that it will slot over one of the raft sticks. Use the table knife or scissors to make another groove all around the mast, about three-quarters up from the bottom end.

Attaching the mast and sail

1 With the two support sticks under the raft pointing toward you, position the mast a few sticks in from one edge. Take two long pieces of twine or string and wrap them around the groove in the mast. Take two ends of the twine or string forward and down and two ends backward and down.

2 Keeping the mast as upright as possible, tie the four ends of twine or string to the support sticks, at both the front and back. (You might need to ask a friend to hold the mast upright while you do this.)

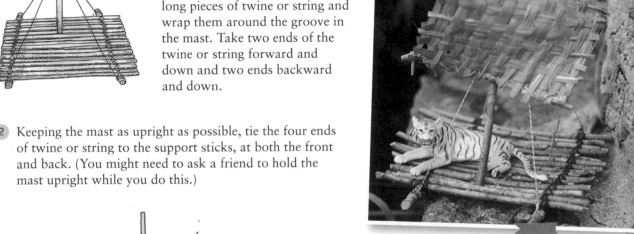

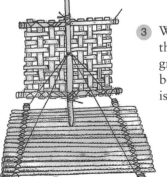

3 When your mast is secure, bind the sail to the mast so that the top sits just above the groove you made for the mast ties. The bottom can be tied to suggest that your sail is billowing in the wind.

4 If you wish, you can also make a flag out of material or paper and attach it to the top of the mast.

5 My Wild Garden and Kitchen

The English saying "To clear away the cobwebs" isn't to do with spiders and their webs. It's about getting outside, breathing in fresh air, and taking exercise. Sometimes, if homework is dull or the television room is stuffy, going into the garden will blow away the cobwebs; you'll feel refreshed. Out in the wild and in the garden you can forget about homework and rules.

When you climb a little way up a tree, you can tower over adults, and your view of the landscape is different too. This chapter is packed with exciting projects for your backyard—whether you are an enthusiastic bug hunter, bird watcher, or star-gazer—as well as lots of delicious recipes to try with wild ingredients that you've foraged in the countryside.

Garden Birds

Attracting wild birds to your garden is very rewarding and may help reverse the trend of declining populations of some common species. Sometimes you may notice leaves, lawn, or patios covered in lots of bird droppings; use this as a possible bird-nest marker—look up and check it out. Swifts bond nest materials together with saliva and nest in walls or under eaves. House martins (*Delichon urbicum*) and house sparrows (*Passer domesticus*) also like nesting in buildings.

GO BIRD WATCHING

The advantage of bird watching in your garden is that birds can become quite tame if you feed them regularly. It isn't very nice when a herring gull (*Larus argentatus*) or American gull (*Larus smithsonianus*) swoops down and steals your ice cream—birds are clever scavengers; however, in the garden, you choose to provide the food and there is usually a bush, tree, bench, or window ledge for birds to perch on.

Make use of bird guides or phone apps to help locate good local viewing spots. Wasteland where plants are left to self-seed and unkempt cemeteries, where in the fall (autumn) trees are laden with berries, are often good places to try. Find out if there are any local online bird blogs for young people and then you will know which species to look for. You may even like to start a blog using your garden bird observation notes. There are lots of different species of birds, but here is a little information about starlings and magpies, two bird species that display some fascinating behaviors.

Blue tit

STARLINGS These birds were introduced to North America in the 19th century by a group called the *American Acclimatization Society*. This group, founded in New York, was dedicated to introducing European flora and fauna to North America. It is rumored that Bronx resident Eugene Schieffelin wanted to introduce every bird mentioned by the writer William Shakespeare to North America. Schieffelin began his quest by releasing 60 starlings in Central Park and now there are millions of starlings in North America. Whether the Eugenie Schieffelin and Shakespeare story is true or not, a starling is mentioned in Shakespeare's *Henry IV Part I* (Act I, Scene iii)—"*Nay, I'll have a starling shall be taught to speak.*"

Starlings, which are indeed excellent mimics, are very common city birds and often found in big, noisy flocks. In the fall (autumn) starlings form the most amazing clouds in the sky. If you've seen Alfred Hitchcock's scary movie *The Birds*, the sight of starlings in cloud formation may bring back memories of that movie. This synchronized sky ballet or murmuration may feel eerie and very out of the ordinary to watch, but it is a natural spectacle. In the United Kingdom starlings gather at the end of summer and join starlings migrating from colder countries such as Russia. Starling murmuration is a real groupie act. During the day

Magpie

Grow Your Own Mistletoe

Mistletoe (*Viscum album*) seeds are spread by birds, but young naturalists can have a go at seeding mistletoe too. Mistletoe has interesting interactions with some insects, birds, mammals, and fungi, as well as the host tree on which it grows. In fact, it forms its own mini ecosystem. In the United Kingdom, the aptly named mistle thrush (*Turdus viscivorus*) gets its common name from its love of mistletoe berries. In North America the botanical name for mistletoe is *Phoradendron*, which comes from the Greek words "thief" and "tree." This is clever because mistletoe is a parasite and hitchhikes a ride on the host tree—it's a tree thief.

To seed mistletoe, push the sticky seeds from the white berries as far as you can into the bark of a tree in your garden or a local wild tree. Mistletoe seeds are naturally sticky. Be patient. Fingers crossed that you will know where to find mistletoe in the years to come. The more berries you can find to do this with, the greater your chance of success. Always wash your hands after seeding mistletoe.

the groups of starlings divide as they forage for food, but then re-group at night before roosting. The sky turns completely black as the birds fly in swirling clouds in unison, copying the exact movement of the bird next to them. The best time to see this is at twilight. The starlings sweep into the most amazing shapes before flying down and roosting in the trees.

MAGPIES The magpie, a member of the Corvidae or crow family, is an opportunistic "see food and eat it" bird. In fact, if there is animal road kill, you can be sure that a member of this family (which also includes crows, ravens, and jays) will be hanging about looking for some fast food. Magpies are frequent visitors to orchards too; they are intelligent birds. In the country, magpies forage for ticks and other insects on the backs of animals. The magpie will pick at wounds on a living animal. This is rather gory. Magpies have other nasty habits too—along with ravens, they will peck out the eyes of newborn or poorly animals and also steal eggs and fledglings from other birds. This is not very pleasant, but on a more positive note magpies do help to keep pest numbers down by eating thousands of insects.

Rose-ringed parakeet

Birds in Danger

Members of the Corvidae family are survivors but, sadly, not all birds are doing well. Some of our best-loved songbirds are disappearing. The cuckoo, for example, is now on the British Red Data List of endangered species. Global warming (see page 18) encourages new species and, unfortunately, some of these non-natives are pests. On the island where I live, greylag geese (*Anser anser*) ruin grazing and crops, and are threatening Hebridean crofting (farming). As a breeding bird, the greylag goose was once considered rare in Scotland. Similarly, the non-native rose-ringed parakeet (*Psittacula krameri*) from India and Asia can be found living in London and the south of England. It is one of the most northerly of wild-living parrots; like the keas of New Zealand, this bird seems to be saying "I don't have to be tropical." The parakeet's smooth green plumage is beautiful—but it competes with native British birds. As the new birds fly in, some of the locals may fly out.

Bird-feeding Roll

In late summer and fall (autumn), try gathering as many different berries, fruits, nuts, and seeds as you can to make a special garden feeder for birds. You can also dry the seeds and store them in envelopes before sowing them in a wild garden in spring. Some very fine seeds are swept away by the wind, but others are eaten or buried by wildlife. This is how plants seed themselves in different places. After Hallowe'en, you might also like to attach a strong hanging loop to your pumpkin or swede lantern and use it as a bird feeder.

WHAT TO USE

- ✔ 2–3 handfuls of wild fall (autumn) berries and fruits (e.g. haws, hips, rowan berries, sloes, and elderberries)
- ✔ Large handful of wild seeds and nuts
- ✔ Small tray
- ✔ Scissors
- ✔ Empty cardboard tube (such as a kitchen or toilet paper roll)
- ✔ 2 thin, straight twigs, about 6in (15cm) in length and no more than ½in (1cm) thick
- ✔ 4 pieces of string, each 20in (50cm) in length
- ✔ Table knife
- ✔ Jar of smooth peanut butter or coconut oil

WHAT TO DO

1. Put the berries, fruits, nuts, and seeds on a small tray.

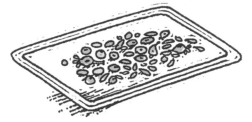

2. Use the scissors to make two tiny snips opposite each other at each end of the cardboard tube (about ¾in/2cm from the ends). That makes four snips in total.

3. Gently push a twig through the opposite holes so that there is an equal amount of twig poking out each side of the tube.

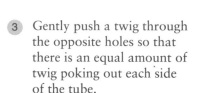

4. Tie a length of string to the end of each twig and then tie the opposite strings together to make two hanging loops.

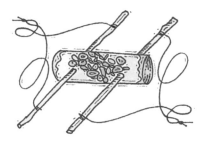

5 Use the knife to spread a thin layer of peanut butter over the tube and then carefully roll this in the berries, fruits, nuts, and seeds. You may need to use your finger to gently push larger seeds and berries into the peanut butter. Make sure the string doesn't get stuck to the tube.

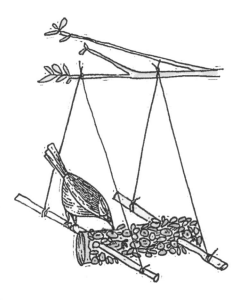

6 Hang the roll from a branch or bird table near a window. Then watch the birds snacking on the wild food you've provided. You could also stick some clumps of light seeds (e.g. dock or sorrel) to the tube, but make sure they aren't too heavy or they will fall off.

Variation

SPREAD THE IDEA—ON A FIR CONE

Look for some big fir cones in the woods. Don't worry if they are damp and tightly shut; left to sunbathe, the cones will open up. Tie a length of strong string around the top of the fir cone and make a hanging loop. Push lashings of coconut oil, lard, or peanut butter into the gaps in the open cone and then push wild seeds and berries into the fat—this is messy but fun. Hang the cones on a branch and keep watch for feathered visitors.

Iced Wildness

In the fall (autumn), you can collect hips, haws, seeds, and nuts to freeze and then feed them to the hungry birds in winter. If you also add some colorful leaves to your sphere of wildness, you'll remember the pretty colors of fall as the ice slowly melts on a winter's day.

WHAT TO USE

- ✔ Small bowl
- ✔ Orange or lemon (fruit) net
- ✔ Berries, hips, haws, small pieces of cone, nuts, and seeds
- ✔ Colorful leaves (optional)
- ✔ Water
- ✔ Piece of string, about 20in (50cm) in length
- ✔ Large bowl of warm water

WHAT TO DO

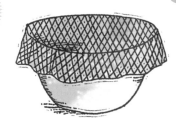

1 Line the small bowl with the unopened end of the fruit net. The bowl needs to be small enough for the net to cover the inside and leave 2–2¼in (5–6cm) hanging over the rim.

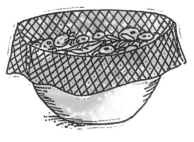

2 Fill the bowl with fall (autumn) berries, cones, nuts, and seeds, plus some colorful leaves if you wish.

Wild Rose Petals

Dry some rose petals in a warm place and then grind them in a liquidizer to use in cooking. You can add a pinch of ground wild rose petals to cake recipes and ask your friends to guess what the added flavor is. In the Middle East rosewater is often sprinkled on meat and powdered rose is scattered over yogurt—you could try this too (see opposite to learn how to make flower water).

Variation

FROZEN BERRY CUBES

You can also freeze some berries with a little water in an ice-cube tray. To feed the birds out of season, put the berry ice cubes on a winter bird table.

3 Pour some water into the bowl until it's three-quarters full. As water freezes, its properties change and it takes up more space—a sneaky science lesson. If you fill the bowl to the brim with water, it may crack as the water expands.

4 Pop the bowl in the freezer for 2 to 3 hours or until it has frozen.

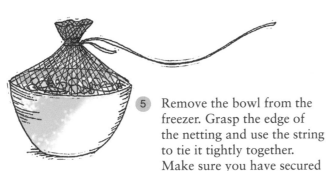

5 Remove the bowl from the freezer. Grasp the edge of the netting and use the string to tie it tightly together. Make sure you have secured the netting well and that the length of string is long enough to hang the ball from a tree.

6 Quickly pop the bowl in and out of a large bowl of warm water—this will loosen the netting from the sides of the smaller bowl.

7 Lift the frozen ball out of the bowl and pop it back in the freezer until you are ready to hang it from a tree.

 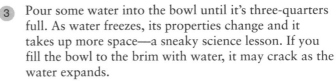

Wild Flower Water

Non-native *Rosa rugosa* is perfect for making flower water, but you can use garden roses or gorse flowers too. Preserving the scent of the Damask rose (*Rosa damascena*) can be traced back to biblical times. Shake the petals well after you've picked them to ensure any visiting insects don't end up in your flower water.

Collect a small basket of rose or gorse petals. Place the petals in a saucepan and add just enough water to cover them. Warm the water over a low heat. Don't let the water boil (lots of big, fast bubbles), but simmer (tiny bubbles) for about 45 minutes until the petals lose their color. Cover the pan with a lid and leave the water to cool. Strain the scented water through a sieve into a jug and then pour into a clean screw-top bottle or jar. Label your wild flower water and store it in the refrigerator.

When you're hot, you can cool yourself down by splashing a little rosewater on your wrists or face. You can also freeze the rose petals to capture the roses' scent. You could make some rosewater in winter, which would bring back lovely summer memories whenever you open the bottle.

Tiny Garden Creatures

Children are usually closer to the ground than adults and this gives you lots of opportunities for wild exploration that adults may miss out on. At ground level in your garden there are plenty of tiny creatures to spy on, including spiders, woodlice, slugs, snails, and earthworms—it's a wonderful world in miniature.

THE CAPTIVATING WORLD OF SPIDERS

Both spiders and insects are invertebrates (i.e. they have no backbone), but spiders are not classified as insects. Instead, spiders, of which there are thousands of species, are categorized as arachnids. A spider has two main body parts: a combined head and thorax (called the cephalothorax) and an abdomen. The cephalothorax has eyes, mouthparts (but no antennae), and four pairs of legs, making eight legs in total (insects only have six legs). A spider has eight eyes, arranged in two rows of four, on the front of the cephalothorax. To the front are small legs called pedipalps or palps, which spiders use to grab prey or mate (to reproduce). The palps are larger in male spiders, but the female is the bigger spider. Spiders hatch out from eggs and then molt (shed) their exoskeletons (external skeletons) as they grow.

Spiders help farmers by eating the insects that damage crops and do a good job keeping our homes and schools free of pests too. Their method of killing isn't pleasant, however: spiders kill by injecting a substance that paralyzes the insect and then they suck out its insides. The Brazilian wandering spider *Phoneutria* is definitely one to avoid. Its scientific name comes from the Greek word for murderess, which sums up its bite too. This spider is nocturnal (a night-worker) and during the day hides in cars and houses or in shipments of bananas. When disturbed the spider will bite. Young naturalists don't need to worry, though, because they can learn about the villains, as well as the good spider guys. Most species of spider enjoy their own company, but some are sociable and build webs together to catch communal prey.

Robert the Bruce and the Cave Spider

The legend of Robert the Bruce, medieval King of Scots, and the spider is famous. After being defeated by the English, King Robert went into hiding in a cave, where he watched a spider trying to build a web. The spider fell down time and time again, but persisted at the task. Finally, the spider managed to stick a strand of silk to the cave wall and was able to weave a web. Robert the Bruce was inspired by the little spider's determination and, with the help of his army, beat the English at the Battle of Bannockburn (in June 1314). More than 500 years later, this fable was told by Sir Walter Scott in *Tales of a Grandfather* (1827). Tenacity—or sticking power—is the message of this spider tale: If at first you don't succeed, try, try, and try again.

SPIDER WEBS Spiders weave webs at night to catch prey. Spinning a web is a long process which uses lots of energy; however, spiders are good at preserving energy by guzzling their own webs. Spiders' webs are camouflaged to blend into the countryside, but they need to be alert because predators such as wasps, ants, and small reptiles and mammals, especially shrews, enjoy snacking on spiders. Birds enjoy spider

Take a photograph of
a dew-covered web.

Make a
Cobweb Card

A clever photographer snaps a cobweb while it's still coated in dew or rain drops. Very early in the morning (after you've run barefoot through the dew) is a brilliant time for you to try to do this. Later in the day you could spray a cobweb with water instead, and then take a photograph. Spiders' webs can look hauntingly beautiful on foggy fall (autumn) mornings. This project traps a real spider's web on a piece of card. Remember that a small creature has made the web so it's not kind to do this often. The story of Robert the Bruce and the spider, however, tells us that a spider is a determined critter and will rebuild its web.

Find a silky spider's web without a spider or any of its food (prey) trapped in the web. Hold a piece of white card (measuring about 6 x 6in/15 x 15cm) behind the web and use a pair of tweezers to carefully pull the web into the center of the card. Spray the card with hairspray and leave to dry.

snacks too. I once watched a spider weave a web on my study window. I marveled at its acrobatic agility. Some days later, a hungry starling skidded to a glass emergency stop and gobbled up the spider. The beautiful web, made from light but incredibly strong spider silk, was smashed. Through the web I was able to watch a layer of the food chain in action.

The extremely fine silk used by spiders to make ballooning webs is known as gossamer. In the 18th century, Frenchman François Xavier Bon de Saint Hilaire demonstrated that fabric could be spun from spider silk. He boiled spider cocoons, extracting the threads with combs to make socks and gloves. A gossamer thread may be made from as many as 100 twisted threads. Some ladies' brands of hosiery include the word gossamer.

BE A GARDEN BUG HUNTER

There are lots of other tiny creatures to look out for in your backyard. Here are a few experiments to help you observe them at close quarters.

HELP SOME BUGS MOVE HOUSE Arrange three to four small, clean, recycled food containers in a shoebox or a small box with a lid. Fill each half of the containers with a different habitat, e.g. white and black shredded paper, dry and wet leaves, wet and dry moss, damp bark, dry grass, and dry and wet soil. Catch a few tiny insects that don't jump—woodlice are ideal—and pop them in the box. Make some holes in the lid of the box with a screwdriver or tapestry needle, and leave the woodlice to choose their favorite home. Come back in an hour or two and see which homes the woodlice have chosen.

Where do woodlice
prefer to live?

MAKE A BUG ATTRACTOR Bugs are attracted to sugar and this rather messy project will allow you to look at them with a magnifying glass. In a small bowl mix a ripe banana with a little brown sugar and leave it for 20 minutes. Find a small log or branch and then smear this with the banana mix. Check up on your experiment a little later to see if there are any visiting insects. Avoid insects that may sting but, if you want to inspect one more carefully, scoop it up with an old spoon and pop it in a glass jar with a bottle cap of water, a stick, and some juicy green leaves. Put the lid on the jar or use some baking parchment secured with a rubber band. Use a fork to poke some holes through the jar cover to ensure the insect has fresh air. Don't keep an insect prisoner for very long and release it where you found it.

Attracting bugs with bananas.

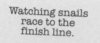

Watching snails race to the finish line.

GARDEN GASTROPOD INVESTIGATION

Snails like damp, shady places. Look for them under plant pots, along the sides of rotting wood, at the base of walls, and under large leaves. Snails have a homing instinct, which means that crafty gardeners who throw snails into a neighbor's garden may find that the same snails return to eat their plants instead. Finding snails isn't always easy. If you keep your snails for more than 24 hours, make sure that the soil is damp and feed them fresh greenery such as grasses, chickweed, or dandelion leaves. Here are a couple of activities to try with snails:

HAVE A GASTROPOD RACE First prepare a racetrack by spraying a tray or plate with some water to help the snails to glide. Use a twig or pen to mark the start and finish lines. Find two snails. Squish some berry juice over one shell so you can tell the snails apart. If you have more than two snails racing, then you could mark the shells with numbered stickers. Set the snails at the start line and wait—the race will take place at a snail's pace. You might want to entice your snails to the finish line with some chickweed. Look out for slimy tracks.

Studying snails in their holiday camp.

BUILD A SNAIL HOTEL Find a clear plastic bottle with a screw top and cut a small rectangular opening on one side of the bottle (make cuts on three sides and leave the door hinge intact). Make air holes with a fork. Fill the bottle base (on the opposite side of the door) with damp soil and fresh greenery. Put a snail (or two if you are using a large bottle) inside the hotel, close the door (with tape if necessary) and watch for a day or two. Remember to release the snail back into the wild.

WIGGLY WORMS

Segmented worms, which don't have legs or a hard skeleton, are divided into many tiny segments. They are in the phylum *Annelida*. There are lots of worm species, but only annelids have linked rings. Some worms can even survive if a ringed section is damaged. There are three main groups of annelids: the earthworms (*Oligochaeta*) and their relatives, the leeches, and a large group that lives in the ocean called *Polychaetes*. Ocean worms swim or crawl, while terrestrial worms wriggle about and hide in "self-build" burrows. Annelids move by contracting their tiny, ring-like segments. The earthworm has two pairs of bristly hairs (called setae) on each segment that help it grip the soil. It moves by stretching and narrowing its body. The head of a worm is found at the end closest to its swollen, non-segmented band, which is called a clitellum. The earthworm breathes through its mucus-coated skin.

Earthworms have light- and touch-sensitive organs (known as receptor cells) to distinguish differences in light and feel vibrations in the ground. There are giant and small earthworms in the annelid family. The giant Australian Gippsland earthworm (*Megascolides australis*) can grow to 10ft (3m), but is rarely seen because it lives in deep burrows. A far more common garden earthworm is the red wriggler from the *Lumbricus* family. These wrigglers are good at guzzling garden compost. Some researchers believe that these earthworms can eat half their body weight in a day. Earthworms may be pink, white, blue, or even green. Sadly, some earthworms are on the Red Data List of endangered species.

Chickweed and Egg Sandwich

Look out for chickweed (*Stellaria media*) growing in gardens and on wasteland (see page 59 for an I.D. photograph). It's worth learning to identify this weed because you can use the leaves in salads. In a mild winter, you'll find chickweed growing all year round. Wash a handful of leaves well and try adding the chickweed to an egg sandwich. Also search for young dandelion leaves because they are tasty in sandwiches and salads too.

WHY WORMS COME TO THE SOIL SURFACE

You can see where an earthworm has been working in the soil by the cast it leaves on the surface. If you jump up and down on a flower or vegetable bed, an earthworm may pop up. This is because earthworms connect the vibrations with rain and predators. Indeed, researchers have suggested that the patter of raindrops on the soil is similar to mole vibrations and that worms surface in the hope of escaping from worm-guzzling moles. So a good time to collect worms for your wormery (see pages 140–41) is after it has rained. Scientists used to think that earthworms came to the surface to avoid drowning in flooded burrows. However, some soil experts now believe they emerge for migration purposes or to find a mate to reproduce. It is much easier for a worm to move longer distances across the soil surface than underground. Earthworms require moisture, which is why they pop out of the soil when it's raining. In dry weather, earthworms dig deeper into the soil where it is moister.

Hedgehog Alert

In the United Kingdom and parts of Europe, if you are lucky, a hedgehog may visit your garden. In the wild, hedgehogs like to eat earthworms, beetles, and caterpillars. They will also eat millipedes, earwigs, slugs, and snails. In the past, people in the UK would leave bread and milk for visiting hedgehogs to eat. It has, however, since been discovered that hedgehogs are lactose-intolerant, which means they cannot digest milk properly. Instead, you should feed them meat-based foods and offer them water to drink.

A WORM'S LIFE The life of an earthworm is hard. Earthworms must avoid predators on the hunt for a protein-rich meal—a worm—while at the same time scavenging for their own food. Birds, snails, toads, moles, and even foxes like to dine on worms. You may see a robin cock its head and hop up and down, as it tries to encourage an earthworm to come out of its burrow—remember an earthworm can feel the vibrations. When not worrying about what to eat or being eaten, worms also have to be on the look out for a mate to reproduce with. The embryos develop in a cocoon, which is a protective casting that the worm leaves in the soil A cocoon is a warm, safe place, where there is food for the embryos to absorb until they hatch. Like all invertebrates, an earthworm's body processes slow down with falling temperatures. They react to advancing cold weather by burrowing deep in the soil where it is warmer.

WORMS—FRIEND OR FOE? Gardeners like earthworms because they keep the soil healthy by aerating it and producing lots of urine. This is high in nitrogen, which is good for the soil. Worms grab nutrients from decaying waste, which means they can help reduce the amount of organic garbage in the trashcan (bin). You can help worms out by throwing fruit and vegetables, coffee grains, and green manure onto a compost heap. Earthworms like to eat grass clippings and vegetable matter, but not very dry leaves, because most of the goodness in a leaf has gone before it falls from the tree (see *What is Photosynthesis?*, on page 37).

Care for Yourself and Nature

Remember the following safety rules when exploring the wild: always wash your hands after handling anything from the natural world and release any wildlife back into the wild as soon as possible.

Build a Wormery

A worm changes the structure of its environment by creating burrows through which water and oxygen can enter and carbon dioxide leave the soil. Charles Darwin (see page 9) called worms "Nature's Ploughs" because they mix soil and organic matter.

WHAT TO USE

- ✔ Large glass jar or plastic bottle
- ✔ Precision screwdriver or tapestry needle
- ✔ 2 circles of wax (greaseproof) paper (to cover the jar or bottle)
- ✔ Small square of newspaper
- ✔ Water spray
- ✔ Sand, leaves, and moist soil (to fill the wormery)
- ✔ Earthworm
- ✔ Vegetable and fruit peelings, tea leaves, coffee grindings, and salad or wild leaves
- ✔ Rubber bands
- ✔ Black paper and sticky tape

WHAT TO DO

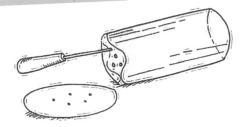

1. If you are using a plastic bottle, cut away the neck and poke 5–6 holes in the bottom using the small screwdriver or tapestry needle. Use the screwdriver or needle to make a few small holes in the circles of wax (greaseproof) paper too.

2 Tear the newspaper into small pieces, spray them with water, and use them to line the bottom of the jar or bottle.

3 Add a layer of sand, followed by a layer of leaves, and then a layer of moist soil. Continue layering in this way until you are within 2¼in (6cm) of the top of the jar or bottle.

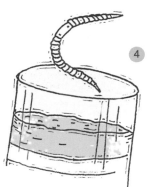

4 Dig up an earthworm. Have a good look at your worm and then pop it in the wormery.

Worm Showers

Bizarrely, there have been reports of earthworms falling from the sky. In 2011 pupils playing soccer at a school in Galashiels, Scotland, were rained on by worms. This weird incident is thought to have been a result of freak weather conditions that caused the worms to be uplifted from a nearby river and dumped on the soccer pitch. A similar worm-raining event was recorded in 1872 in Somerville, Massachusetts. The most recent example of a worm shower was in April 2015 in southern Norway. A biology teacher discovered thousands of earthworms on the snow while out skiing. At first glance he thought that the worms were dead, but they were alive.

5 Put some food such as vegetable and fruit peelings in the jar or bottle, cover the opening with the circles of wax (greaseproof) paper, and then secure with the rubber band.

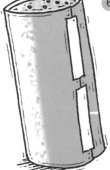

6 Wrap some black paper around the jar or bottle and keep it in place with some sticky tape. (You can also cover the wormery with a lightweight blanket if this is easier.)

7 Place the wormery in a cool, dark place and check each day to see what your earthworm is up to—you'll need to remove the black paper to do this.

8 Release the captive earthworm into the wild when you have studied the patterns it has made in the soil.

Night-time Garden Adventures

If you have a trampoline in the garden, you can have fun "blowing away the cobwebs," but this is also the perfect place to lie back, look up at the night sky, and study the moon and stars. Garden adventures can be special at night too, whether you are gazing at the stars or conducting a moth investigation.

GO STAR-GAZING

Astronomy is the study of space and the objects in it, including the moon and stars. The Babylonians were the first people to write about the stars and the first to notice that they form patterns, which we call constellations (star groups). The Greek astronomer Ptolemy (circa 150 A.D.) wrote about 48 constellations and named them after characters in Greek myths. A constellation is an arrangement of stars that looks like an animal, object, or mythological creature. There are 88 official constellations. Check them out one at a time— different constellations appear in the night sky throughout the year.

FIND ORION AND CASSIOPEIA Today, we still use the names given to the constellations by Ptolemy. Orion is a constellation named after a mythological Greek hunter. Lots of stars make up Orion's shape. Rigel, the brightest star, is found in one of the hunter's legs. One of the easiest of Ptolemy's constellations to spot is Cassiopeia, which is named after the boastful, vain queen from Greek mythology. This constellation is visible all year round in the Northern Hemisphere and its bright stars make the shape of the letter "W."

Cassiopeia is always visible in the Northern Hemisphere.

FIND THE BIG DIPPER The Big Dipper (USA) or The Plough (UK) is easy to identify: it's a group of seven stars and is a good place to begin your star-gazing adventures. The Big Dipper is an asterism, which is part of the constellation Ursa Major. In Latin this means Greater She Bear. According to Native American legend, Ursa Major is lowest in the sky when the bear is looking for a place to lie down for its winter hibernation, and highest in the spring.

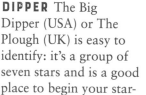
In the Big Dipper, Merak and Dubhe, the two outermost stars, point to the North Star.

To join the Roman army, soldiers had to take an eye test that involved spotting stars in the handle of the Big Dipper. If a Roman solider could spot Alcor, which is brighter than Mizar, he passed the test to serve as an archer. Dubhe and Merak, the two outermost stars of the Big Dipper, point to The North Star or Polaris. Amateur astronomers call these stars the pointers—if you extend a line about six times the distance between Dubhe and Merak and can't see a bright star, The North Star, you've not found the Big Dipper. The Plough or Big Dipper rotates counterclockwise around the North Star, which means it can appear "upside down" or "sideways" on. Some people call this group of stars the saucepan. This asterism appears on the Cherokee peace flag and Alaska state flag.

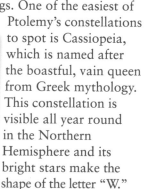

FIND THE NORTH STAR This star sits above the North Pole and is the only star that doesn't move— other stars circle around it. True north lies directly under this star—in times of old, sailors used this star to chart their direction of sail. When you spend time star- and moon-gazing, you too, can be guided by nature. Natural navigation is not only out-of-door fun but useful too.

WHEN TO GO STAR-GAZING Big starry skies are best viewed far away from the glare of streetlights in cities and towns, which can cause light pollution. You can check on a dark sky website to find the best local place to star-gaze, but a dark back garden or local park is often a good place to start. You can, of course, see stars with the naked eye in cities, but you'll get a better view if you go further from street lighting.

Winter is a good time for family constellation viewing because the sun sets early. You may even be lucky enough to see a meteor (shooting star) or the brighter planets: Jupiter, Mars, and Venus. Venus is the brightest star in the Solar System and can be seen during the day if you know where to look. When Venus is to the west of the Sun, she rises before the Sun and is known as the Morning Star. When Venus is to the east, she shines just after sunset, and is then called the Evening Star.

Daytime Sky-gazing

Although the most exciting star-gazing takes place at night, which may be restricted by bedtimes in the summer, cool things also happen in the sky during the day. Depending on its phase, the Moon may still be visible in daylight hours, while a solar eclipse is always exciting to watch. This occurs when the Sun and Moon are aligned with each other in such a way that (from the Earth) the Moon appears to block out the light of the Sun.

GO MOON WATCHING

On a clear night you can see the Moon with your naked eye. The Moon controls the oceans and rules over the tides. You'll notice the Moon's power when the sea races over the sand and destroys your sandcastles. Neil Armstrong was the first man to step on the Moon on July 21, 1969. Only twelve people have set foot on the Moon and their footprints are still there. We can still see these footprints because, unlike the Earth, the Moon has no atmosphere. If you look at the surface of the Moon through binoculars, you may see craters, pits, and scars caused by large pieces of rock hitting its surface billons of years ago.

WHY DOES THE MOON SHINE? The Moon acts like a mirror and reflects sunlight. From Earth we can see the near side of the Moon; the other side is the far side. The amount of the Moon we can see depends on the angle of the Moon as it goes around the Earth. This explains why on a full moon you can walk by moonlight and do not need a flashlight, whereas at other times of the month the moonshine is just a small slither of light. If you look at the Moon when it is nearly full, you'll see dark areas known as seas or oceans. They have Latin names beginning with *mare*, but are made of lava, not seawater.

The Northern Lights

A curtain of green and red, dancing lights in the sky at night is called the Northern Lights. On the northern British isle of Orkney, the lights are called The Merry Dancers. Historically, folklore associated seeing the display with disaster and war. Galileo Galilei called the lights the *Aurora Borealis*, after Aurora the Roman goddess of morning. The lights occur when electrically charged particles from the Sun (a solar wind) hit the Earth's magnetic field. I am fortunate because I live on an island in northern Scotland, where on a clear night magnificent greens and reds light up the sky at certain times of the year.

Moon-gazer Facts

✳ Galileo was the first person to make moon maps showing the moon's changing phases. It takes 27.3 days for the moon to orbit the Earth, but 29.5 days for it to go through its eight phases: New Moon, Waxing Crescent, First Quarter, Waxing Gibbous, Full Moon, Waning Gibbous, Last Quarter, and Waning Crescent. This is known as a lunar month. Check the moon's phase on a lunar calendar (see *Resources*, on page 157) before moon-gazing.

✳ A super or perigee moon occurs when the moon is at its closest point to Earth in its orbit. The most amazing spring tides take place with a perigee moon. This is a great time to forage seaweed or spy on sealife in the sub-tidal zone.

✳ A blue moon is the second full moon in a calendar month. The expression "Once in a blue moon" suggests it is a rare occurrence, but it happens on average once every three years.

✳ Local names for a full moon vary between nationalities. The September full moon is often referred to as The Harvest or Corn Moon, probably because staple foods are gathered in September in the Northern Hemisphere. This moon is the one closest to the fall (autumn) equinox, which can very occasionally fall in October. One of my favorite moons is June's Strawberry, Rose, or Flower Moon, which occurs when strawberries are ripe and roses are in bloom.

Star and Moon Gazing-and-lazing

Get outside, lie back on a blanket, look up at the night sky, and see what you can spot. Here is some gold-star advice for successful star- and moon-gazing:

✳ The best time to star and moon gaze-and-laze is before the moon is full, so check your lunar calendar.

✳ Keep cozy—you may like to wrap yourself up to your neck in a sleeping bag and wear a warm hat.

✳ Dusk is the best time to start star-gazing because your eyes will adjust to the darkening sky.

✳ Take a star chart or phone app (and flashlight to read it) and a warm drink in a thermos flask.

✳ A flashlight with a red lens makes star-gazing easier.

✳ Begin with a pair of binoculars. (Make sure you know how to use them, as it's tricky to learn in the dark.) If you want to become a star-gazing geek, buy a telescope, but only when you're certain you like being outside at night—it can get chilly.

✳ The stars you see will change throughout the year.

✳ Once you know how to spot a constellation as quickly as you can spy a shooting star (meteor), it's time to turn your gaze and learn about another.

✳ Be prepared to learn your constellations slowly. Think of it like adding pieces to a difficult jigsaw puzzle.

✳ Track your star-gazing in a journal, noting the constellation name, place seen, and date.

✳ Vacations under canvas are a good way to explore the sky at night because you are usually far from city lights.

✳ The sky is really clear after snow.

✳ If you live near a beach, or are on a seaside trip, you can use pebbles to mark the constellations on the sand.

AFTER DARK MOTH INVESTIGATIONS

Looking for moths is easier than searching for butterflies because moths are attracted by light. Any light will do; you've probably seen them fluttering around your bedroom lamp. They are also attracted by the scent of ripe fruits and sugar, which they like to feed on. At night, if you leave a porch light on and the door open, you probably won't have to wait long before a passing moth is attracted to the light. If you want to spy on moths, you need to provide something for them to rest on. A simple project is to peg a white sheet on a washing line, make sure any outside lights are turned off, and then shine a bright flashlight at the sheet—wait and see which moths flutter by. You can also attract moths by mixing something delicious for them to eat. This is known as sugaring. Here are a couple of sugaring projects for moth investigators:

HOST A MOTHS' DINNER PARTY Loop a strong rubber band around the center of a tennis ball so it is taut. Tie one end of a 40-in (100-cm) length of craft string to the rubber band. Loop the length and secure with a knot so that the ball can hang from the string. Over a low heat, warm ¾ cup (200ml) of fruit juice and 3 tablespoons of brown sugar in a small pan until the sugar dissolves. Carefully pour the syrupy mixture into a small bowl and pop in the ball. Leave the ball to soak for 15 minutes, turning it occasionally to ensure it is well coated. Take the bowl into the garden (to avoid sticky drips) and hang the ball in a sheltered place in a tree or bush—watch out for night-time visitors.

MAKE SOME SUGARED MOTH STRIPS Soak five or six 10–20in (25–50cm) lengths of rag in the fruit syrup (as above). Squeeze out the excess syrup and pop the strips on a tray. Peg the strips on a washing line or hang them over the branches of a tree. Wait until after dark and check which species of moths have invited themselves to dine at your moths' dinner party. You can also use a pastry brush to paint the syrupy mixture onto the bark of a garden tree.

If you leave a porch light on and the door open, you won't have to wait long before a passing moth is attracted to the light

Encourage moths to your garden with some sugary treats.

My Wild Kitchen

In the past cooks prepared meals using seasonal ingredients; only the diet of the rich might include imported foods. Our ancestors would think ahead and dry or preserve some victuals (foods) to eat out of season, just as we store food in a freezer today. Squirrels hide food that they've picked in times of plenty for the winter when wild food is sparse. Nuts gathered in the fall (autumn) are an important source of protein. In 1995, on the Scottish island of Colonsay, archaeologists found a pit of burnt hazelnut shells from about 9,000 years ago. This tells us that our ancestors squirreled away food when it was in season—similarly, you'll need to pick wild ingredients when they are available. Wild food is *always* seasonal.

NATURE'S BOUNTIFUL LARDER

In the woods, with expert I.D, you can pick fungi (see pages 42–43) in the fall (autumn), while in spring you may smell wild garlic (see page 29) before you see it. Nettles may sting, but the young leaves are nutritious and tasty. Wild garlic, dandelions, and other wild leaves can all be used to make a pesto or salad. Wild and sea rocket, and mustard leaves, add a punchy flavor. You might also want to snack on hedgerow fruits or pick them to use in your wild kitchen. Don't forget that seeds can be eaten too. If you're foraging by the coast, you can gather seaweed at and beyond the splash zone: sea kale, the oraches, marsh samphire, and rock samphire (see page 89). As you learn to cook with wild ingredients, your confidence will grow. For example, you'll be able to look at a quince and know it isn't an apple. The next step is to take your quince into the kitchen and learn how to cook it— from a book or app for wild cooks.

USEFUL EQUIPMENT FOR WILD COOKS

If you like cooking with wild ingredients such as flower petals and dried seaweed, it is really useful to have a set of digital scales. The scales will help you weigh small quantities very accurately. These are very handy, especially if you enjoy baking. Food dehydrators are not expensive and are great for drying wild herbs, mushrooms, seaweeds, petals, and berries. It is less expensive to heat a food dehydrator than turn an oven on for hours— drying wild food sometimes takes a long time.

Wild Cooking Tips

* Never pick more than a sixth of any wild ingredient.

* Always check that you have the landowner's permission before gathering food.

* Remember: *Don't Munch on a Hunch* (see page 14) and make sure that your "Yes, Can Eat, I.D. Certain" is 100 percent accurate.

* Read the recipe through twice before you begin. Check whether you have to prepare any of the ingredients first before starting the recipe.

* Always wash your hands after foraging and before cooking.

Sterilizing Jars and Bottles

If you're making recipes such as the *Meadowsweet Diluting Syrup* (see pages 152–53) or wild fruit jam or curds, you'll need to sterilize the jars or bottles they are stored in. To sterilize a jar or bottle, wash the glass (and lid) in some hot, soapy water and place upside-down in a preheated oven (250°F/120°C/Gas ½) for 30 minutes. You can also sterilize jars in a dishwasher.

Dried Wild Mushrooms

You'll be surprised how mushrooms shrink when they are dried. The flavor is, however, concentrated which means that you won't need to use very many. Finely ground dried wild mushrooms can be used for seasoning and also make a good stock for soup.

WHAT TO DO

1. Brush the wild mushrooms well, but don't wash them. If they are very dirty, wipe them with a damp cloth.

2. Lay the clean mushrooms on a baking or dehydrator tray.

3. Set the oven or dehydrator to the lowest setting. This means that the drying process may take a little longer. If you have a range cooker, you can dry the mushrooms on trays on the back of the range. You can also dry them on a shelf above a warm boiler. They must be very dry. Test one—it should snap, not bend.

4. Store the dried mushrooms in an airtight container or grind into a dust and store in a jar with a lid.

Wild Garlic Parcels

These wild parcels are delicious cold but you could also serve them warm. Steam the parcels or cook them in a little broth until they are heated through.

WHAT TO USE

- ✔ 1oz (25g) easy-cook couscous
- ✔ About ¼ cup (50ml) boiled water (read the packet instructions)
- ✔ Large carrot
- ✔ 2 teaspoons wild seeds
- ✔ 1 tablespoon hummus
- ✔ 24 washed wild garlic leaves
- ✔ Toothpicks (cocktail sticks) or extra wild garlic leaves or chives

Makes approx. 12

WHAT TO DO

1. Put the couscous in a bowl and carefully pour in the very hot, but not boiling, water. Cover the bowl and wait for about 5 minutes until the couscous has absorbed the water. Fluff up the grains with a fork.

2. Chop any wild garlic stalks into small pieces. Peel the carrot and grate one big tablespoon.

3. Add the stalks, grated carrot, seeds, and hummus to the couscous and mix together with a fork. The mixture should be moist, but still bind together.

4. Lay two garlic leaves flat, one on top of the other, shiny sides down. Place a heaped teaspoon of the mixture on the top leaf, at the end closest to you. Leave the edges clear of mixture.

5. Gently roll up the leaves to make a parcel and secure by pushing a toothpick (cocktail stick) through the center. If you like doing fiddly things, you can tie the parcel with strips of wild garlic or chives.

Picking wild garlic

Blackberry and Sorrel Leathers

Apple helps a fruit leather mix to set and its addition means that you won't have to forage too many berries. Fruit leathers are easy to make but take time to dry out. They are worth waiting for.

WHAT TO USE

- ✔ 1¼lb (600g) washed blackberries
- ✔ Large cooking apple (approx. 10½oz/300g), peeled and chopped
- ✔ ⅓ cup (75g) superfine (caster) sugar (to taste)
- ✔ 4 finely chopped sheep sorrel leaves (optional)

Makes approx. 35

WHAT TO DO

1. Cook the blackberries, apple, sugar, and sorrel leaves in a saucepan over a low heat until the apple and blackberries lose their shape. Taste and add more sugar if required. Use a potato masher to bash the ingredients until they are smooth. Leave the mixture to cool.

2. Push the purée through a plastic sieve into a pitcher (jug).

3. The next stage of the recipe can be done in a food hydrator or oven, as follows:

   In a food dehydrator: Pour the purée as thinly as possible (i.e. no thicker than ¼in/5mm) over 3–4 racks lined with non-stick baking paper. The drying time will depend on the thickness of the mixture and the machine model.

   In an oven: Pour the purée as thinly as you can onto baking trays lined with baking paper (or oiled foil). Bake at the oven's lowest temperature for 12–24 hours until the purée is dry and peels away from the paper (or foil). Watch the color as the purée begins to dry out—you may need to prop open the oven door to keep the temperature down.

4. Leave the leathers to cool before peeling off the paper or foil. Cut the leathers into thin strips, rolling them into coils if you wish. Store in an airtight container.

Wild Cook's Note: If the leathers are still damp in the center, leave them to dry for a little longer in the dehydrator or oven. The leathers are done when they are gummy, but not sticky.

Sheep Sorrel

Sheep sorrel (*Rumex acetosella*) is a useful herb to cook with. Bees, butterflies, caterpillars and small insects feed on sorrel. It has a long cooking and interesting medical history. In mild winters you may find sorrel growing all year round. Its leaf looks like a tiny, smooth dock leaf, but it has an arrow mark where the leaf joins the stalk. The V-mark looks like a bride's wedding train. In summer meadows, red sorrel seeds can be found dancing in the breeze among buttercups (*Ranunculus* spp.). If you pick a buttercup and hold it under a friend's chin— and it reflects the color yellow—then folklore says your friend likes butter. Sorrel tastes sour, but in a Haribo-sour, yummy kind of way. Scottish children used to chew on sorrel when they were thirsty. In areas where lemons didn't grow, and before they were available in stores, sorrel was used to add tartness. You can dry sorrel leaves, grind them in a liquidizer, and store the powder in a jar to sprinkle like a dried herb or perhaps to make *Sorrel Sherbet* (see page 57).

Sorrel and Wild Chive Paneer

This recipe makes a small, but rich, round of soft cheese. You need a juicer to make this cheese. You'll find wild chives (*Allium schoenoprasum*) from late spring to summer. You could try adding a pinch of finely ground dried *Rosa rugosa* petals (see page 134), if you'd like to try a scented cheese. You can replace the chives in the recipe with a sprinkling of dried seaweed or other finely chopped fresh herbs if you wish.

WHAT TO USE

✔ ⅔ cup (150ml) milk
✔ 3 tablespoons sheep sorrel juice (about a medium-sized bowl of leaves)
✔ Small circle of muslin
✔ 1 coffeespoon chopped chives

Makes 1 cheese

WHAT TO DO

1. Wash the sorrel leaves and push them through a juicer. Younger children may need some adult help to do this.

2. Measure the milk into a pitcher (jug) and add the 3 tablespoons of sorrel juice.

3. Put the pitcher in a warm place and cover with a clean napkin. Forget about it for 24 hours.

4. The milk will curdle (go lumpy), splitting into curds and whey. Sorrel takes longer than bottled rennet to curdle milk, so don't worry if it takes a while.

5. Strain the whey thorough a plastic sieve lined with a circle of muslin. Use the back of a teaspoon to push through the whey and place the curds in a small bowl.

6. Carefully mix the chopped chives into the curds and the paneer is ready to eat. You can use the leftover whey if you are making pastry or bread.

Wild Scotch Pancakes

In summer you can add elderflowers, meadowsweet, or rose petals to pancakes. Tiny bilberries will splatter color as they cook, while in the fall (autumn), seeds will add crunchiness to these soft and fluffy pancakes.

WHAT TO USE

- ✔ 20 *Rosa rugosa* petals
- ✔ ¾ cup (100g) self-rising flour
- ✔ 1 teaspoon baking powder
- ✔ 1 tablespoon superfine (caster) sugar (to taste)
- ✔ 1 US large (UK medium) egg
- ✔ About ½ cup (125ml) milk
- ✔ Butter, for greasing

Makes 20 (depending on size)

WHAT TO DO

1. As you collect the petals, shake them well to remove any insects. When you are in the kitchen, brush the petals with a pastry brush to make sure that there aren't any tiny bug visitors.

2. Sift the flour and baking powder into a mixing bowl and add the sugar.

3. Make a hole in the center of the flour and sugar, and break the egg in the hole.

4. Place a damp cloth under the bowl to keep it still, then use a small whisk to beat the ingredients together and slowly mix in the milk.

5. Beat the batter until it is smooth and without lumps. You may not need all of the milk—the mix needs to be a thick, not runny, batter.

6. Heat a knob of butter in a skillet (frying pan)—do not let it brown—and drop a scant tablespoonful of the batter into the pan (it may be easier to put the batter into a measuring cup and slowly pour the batter into the pan from the cup).

7. When the pancake puffs up and starts to bubble, drop a rose petal into the center and then flip it over with a spatula. Cook for another 30 seconds or so until the pancake puffs up and the underside is golden. Remove the rose pancake from the pan.

8. Repeat until you have used all of the batter, adding extra butter to the pan as needed. Wrap the pancakes in a clean dishtowel to keep warm.

Rosa rugosa

This plant is native to eastern Asia, but is replacing native rose species throughout northern Europe. On the positive side, its scented pink flowers attract bumblebees. *Rosa rugosa* has larger summer petals and fall (autumn) hips than the hedgerow dog rose (*Rosa canina*). Both species of rose grow in hedgerows, sand dunes, cliffs, roadsides, and waste ground. If you wish to cook with roses, pick the petals and not the whole rose, and shake the flower well to allow any insects to re-house locally. In the fall, come back for the hips, which you can use in syrups, jellies, chutney, or teas.

Pineapple Weed Tea

For me, gathering, cooking, and eating wild food holds lots of happy childhood memories. In one of his books, the French writer Marcel Proust describes drinking lime blossom tea with an aunt with great fondness: *"Le goût du morceau de madeleine trempé dans le tilleul"*—the taste of a crumb of madeleine soaked in tilleul (lime blossom) tea. Linden or lime blossom, as well as chamomile flowers, are very good for making tea, but you can also use pineapple weed (*Matricaria discoidea*). This weed grows on wasteland and even in car parks, but make sure you pick it where pets haven't relieved themselves. The tiny yellow flower heads smell of pineapple, so it's easy to I.D. The best time to pick herbs for drying is in the morning after the dew has gone, but before the sun gets too hot. You can use fresh or dried pineapple weed. Try adding some freshly picked pineapple buds to a salad.

WHAT TO DO

1. To make your own wild teabag, place the piece of muslin under a small saucer or ramekin dish and draw around the edge. Cut out the circle.

2. Put the dried pineapple weed buds in the center of the circle and tie with the cotton or string. Repeat to make more teabags. (Although you can use coffee filter paper instead of muslin, you can wash and reuse the muslin circles after you've thrown away the used tea.)

3. Put a teabag in a cup and if necessary ask an adult to help you pour in some boiling water. Leave the teabag to steep for at least 5 minutes to allow the flavor to escape. Now enjoy drinking your wild tea—no milk is required, but you may like to add a little honey to sweeten it.

Drying Pineapple Weed

Early in the morning cut some pineapple weed with scissors (this weed has tough stalks). Bunch the stalks together with string. Hang the wild bouquet upside down in a warm, dry place until it is dry. This will take about two weeks. Use scissors to snip off the dried pineapple weed buds and pop them in a jar. Seal with a lid.

Recipe Variation

Add Douglas fir needles for pine tea or short sprigs of fresh wild mint to a cup of boiling water to make peppermint tea. (Look out for a Douglas fir cone—it has three bracts that look like the hind legs and tail of a mouse.)

Bilberry and Sorrel Seed Muffins

Scandinavian cooks crush the seeds of sheep sorrel (*Rumex acetosella*) and add them to bread. The seeds are delicious in muffins too. You could also use poppy seeds (see page 52) or replace the bilberries with blackberries or raspberries.

WHAT TO USE

- ✔ Scant 2½ cups (300g) self-rising flour
- ✔ 1 teaspoon baking powder
- ✔ ½ cup (100g) superfine (caster) sugar
- ✔ 1 tablespoon sheep sorrel seeds
- ✔ Scant ¾ cup (175ml) milk
- ✔ ½ cup (125ml) vegetable oil
- ✔ 1 US large (UK medium) egg
- ✔ 3½oz (100g) bilberries

Makes 12

WHAT TO DO

1. Preheat the oven to 350°F/ 180°C/160°C Fan/Gas 4 and put the muffin cases in a muffin pan.

2. Place the dry ingredients (flour, baking powder, sugar, and sorrel seeds) in a mixing bowl.

3. Measure the milk and oil into a large measuring pitcher (jug) and beat together. Add the egg and mix well.

4. Add the bilberries to the dry ingredients in the bowl and then slowly add the liquid to the dry ingredients. Use a metal spoon to fold the dry and wet mixtures together until "just" mixed.

5. Use a spoon to divide the mixture between the muffin cases.

6. Bake in the oven for 20–25 minutes until golden. Transfer the hot muffins to a cooling rack—they will go soggy if you leave them in the pan to cool.

Meadowsweet Diluting Syrup

When the sun is shining, cut some meadowsweet flower heads. Shake the blossom to leave any insects in their home neighborhood. Earlier in the summer, you can make this cordial with elderflowers. You can also use diluting syrups with gelatin and wild fruits in wild jellies (see *Vitamin C Rich Rosehip Jelly*, opposite).

WHAT TO USE

- ✔ 20 meadowsweet flower heads
- ✔ 4 unwaxed lemons
- ✔ 6 cups (1.2kg) superfine (caster) sugar
- ✔ 5 cups (1.2 liters) water
- ✔ 2oz (55g) citric acid
- ✔ Muslin

Makes 4–5 small bottles

WHAT TO DO

1. Put the meadowsweet flower heads in a clean bucket.

2. Slice the lemons as finely as you can and add the lemon slices to the bucket.

3. Put a big pan on the stovetop and measure the sugar and water into the pan. Cook over a low heat to dissolve the sugar. Stir with a wooden spoon.

4. Add the citric acid to the syrup and stir until it dissolves.

5. Pour the syrup into the bucket over the meadowsweet and lemons. Younger children may need adult help.

Vitamin C Rich Rosehip Jelly

This simple wild jelly is also yummy when made half and half with apple juice.

✔ 14oz (400g) rosehips
✔ 3½ cups (850ml) water
✔ ¼ cup (50g) sugar
✔ About 6 gelatin sheets (follow the directions on the pack and add extra leaves for a firmer set)

Makes 6 individual jellies or 1 large jelly

6 When the syrup has cooled down, carefully bash the meadowsweet a couple of times with a potato masher. This will mix everything together. Cover the bucket with a clean cloth and forget about it for 2–3 days.

7 Ask an adult to help you lift the bucket into a sink. Fill a big measuring pitcher (jug) with the meadowsweet syrup. Strain the flowers and syrup through a sieve lined with muslin into a big pitcher. Repeat until you have strained all of the meadowsweet syrup.

8 Using a pitcher that isn't too heavy, pour the meadowsweet syrup through a funnel into sterilized glass bottles or smaller plastic bottles (see page 146 for advice on sterilizing). Plastic bottles can be frozen (see *Iced Wildness*, on pages 134–35, for advice on water expansion), but leave a 1¼–1½in (3–4cm) gap at the top of the plastic bottles. Smaller bottles are good for small families.

9 Store your meadowsweet syrup in the refrigerator. You can dilute the syrup in drinks or use it in vinaigrettes, or with yogurt, granola, or oatmeal.

1 Rinse the rosehips in some cold water and then put them in a saucepan with the water.

2 Bring the pan to a boil (lots of bubbles), pop a lid on the pan, and lower the heat to a simmer (tiny bubbles) for about an hour.

3 Look at the hips—they should be very soft and tiny hip seeds will be floating on the surface of the juice. Remove the pan from the heat and leave it to cool.

4 If you have a jelly bag, strain the hips through the bag into a bowl overnight. Otherwise, strain them through a plastic sieve into a bowl. Don't hurry the hips along by pushing them through with a spoon, unless you want cloudy jelly.

5 Measure 2½ cups (600ml) of the hip juice into a stainless-steel pan and add the sugar (adjusting to taste). Warm the pan over a low heat to dissolve the sugar.

6 Put the gelatin sheets in a small bowl and cover them with cold water. Set aside until the gelatin feels squidgy (about 3–4 minutes).

7 Remove the soft gelatin and add it to the warm hip juice. Stir well and cook for a minute or so to dissolve the gelatin. Don't let the jelly mix boil.

8 Pour your wild jelly into six small molds or a bigger serving dish. If you are a new hip taster, you may like to try making this jelly with 1¼ cups (300ml) of apple juice and 1¼ cups (300ml) of hip juice.

Blackberry Swirls

Change the fruit swirl with the season. In early summer use wild raspberries or strawberries. In late fall (autumn) you could try sweetened elderberries.

WHAT TO USE

- ✔ ½ cup (125g) unsalted butter
- ✔ ⅓ cup (75g) superfine (caster) sugar
- ✔ 1⅓ cups (180g) all-purpose (plain) flour
- ✔ 1 egg yolk

For the filling
- ✔ ¾ cup (100g) blackberries
- ✔ 1 tablespoon water
- ✔ 1 tablespoon sugar

Makes 30 (depending on size)

WHAT TO DO

1. To make the filling, place the blackberries, water, and sugar in a small saucepan and cook over a low heat until the blackberries collapse and the mixture is thick. Stir the pan as the blackberries cook to make sure they don't stick. Leave to cool.

2. In a mixing bowl cream the butter and sugar together with a wooden spoon. Add the flour and then mix everything together with the egg yolk.

3. Divide the mixture in half. On a floured surface carefully roll out a rectangle of cookie dough measuring about 8 x 6in (20 x 15cm). Pop a larger 16 x 12in (40 x 30cm) rectangle of plastic wrap (clingfilm) under the cookie dough and spread half of the cold blackberry purée over the dough.

4. This is a little tricky: you'll need to work quickly and it may be messy. Roll the cookie mixture up like a jelly (Swiss) roll—using the plastic wrap to help you. You will end up with a sausage-shaped roll of cookie dough in plastic wrap. Repeat these steps using the remaining cookie dough.

5. Refrigerate both rolls of dough for a minimum of 20 minutes (so that they are firm to slice).

6. Preheat the oven to 350°F/180°C/160°C Fan/ Gas 4.

7. Cut ½in (1cm) slices of blackberry swirls and lay them on a non-stick baking tray. Bake for about 10 minutes until the swirls are golden. Keep a watchful eye because they may color quickly.

8. Remove the trays from the oven and leave the swirls to harden on the tray for 2–3 minutes before placing them on a cooling rack.

Blackberries

Late summer and early fall (autumn) are the best months for picking blackberries (*Rubus fruticosus*). There are hundreds of species of blackberries. The juiciest fruit is found at the tip of the lowest cluster and is usually the first to ripen. Pick on into mid-fall as a dare, because folklore says that after the old calendar date of the Feast of St. Michael the Archangel (Old Michaelmas Day—October 11), the Devil spits or urinates on blackberries. Perhaps this is why they are often found at the edge of old graveyards—as a natural deterrent to sheep, but also to keep out the Devil. The barbed stems of the blackberry or bramble were called "lawyers" because they prevent you escaping if they hook onto your clothing.

Dulse and Cheese Scones

Dulse adds a smoky-bacon flavor to food without you having to use a broiler (grill) or skillet (frying pan). If you can't find buttermilk, you can make your own by souring milk with a little lemon juice. Really wild kids forage sheep sorrel leaves and sour the milk with sorrel juice. Don't knead scone dough or your scones will be heavy.

WHAT TO USE

- 1¾ cups (225g) self-rising flour
- 1 teaspoon baking powder
- 2 heaped teaspoons dried ground dulse (see page 87 to find out how to dry seaweed)
- 1½ tablespoons (25g) cold butter
- ¼ cup (25g) grated hard cheese
- Approximately ⅔ cup (150ml) buttermilk

Makes 8

WHAT TO DO

1. Preheat the oven to 425°F/220°C/200°C Fan/Gas 7.

2. Sift the flour, baking powder, and dulse into a bowl. Use your fingers to rub in the butter until it looks like breadcrumbs.

3. Pop a damp cloth under the bowl to stop it moving as you mix. Add the cheese and mix everything together. Stir in enough buttermilk to make a dough.

4. Turn the dough onto a lightly floured surface and roll it out until it is 1¼in (3cm) thick. Use a 2in (5cm) cutter to stamp out 8 scones. Use your hands to shape the last scone.

5. Place the scones onto a non-stick baking tray. Brush with a little buttermilk and bake in the oven for about 10 minutes or until the scones are risen and golden.

6. Put the scones on a cooling rack to cool.

Seaside Sprinkles

You can mix and match any wild seeds in this recipe. If you dry seeds and seaweed, and then store them, you can make seaside sprinkles throughout the year. If you like popping corn, toss some finely ground dried seaweed onto the warm corn for a taste of the sea—it's healthier than salt.

WHAT TO USE

- 2 tablespoons sheep sorrel seeds
- 1 tablespoon finely ground dried dulse (see page 87 to find out how to dry seaweed)
- 1 dessertspoon finely ground dried sea lettuce
- 2 tablespoons black sesame seeds

WHAT TO DO

1. Heat a non-stick skillet (frying pan). When it is hot, add the sorrel seeds and dried seaweed. Dry-roast the mix for 2–3 minutes, stirring all the time.

2. Add the sesame seeds but—beware—the sesame seeds may jump out of the pan. Stand back and stir carefully for a minute to cook all the ingredients together.

3. Turn off the heat and leave the pan to cool. It may not look it, but it will be very hot. Tip your sprinkles into a small container and use them in savory baking or just eat them.

Seashore Omelet

You can use dried seaweed in this omelet if you wish. Dried bladder wrack is tasty with slices of tomato. Tomato and seaweed contain *umami*, which is the newest of the five basic tastes.

WHAT TO USE

- ✔ 1oz (25g) finely chopped fresh sea spaghetti (see page 81)
- ✔ 2 extra large (large) eggs
- ✔ Black pepper (optional)
- ✔ Knob of butter
- ✔ 1 teaspoon dried laver (see page 87 to find out how to dry seaweed)

Makes 1

WHAT TO DO

1. Cook the sea spaghetti in a saucepan of boiling water for 5 minutes and drain well.

2. Break the eggs into a bowl and use a balloon whisk to beat them together. Season with black pepper if you wish.

3. Heat a small omelet pan and add a knob of butter. When the butter foams, add the beaten eggs and cook until the base begins to set.

4. Scatter the sea spaghetti and dried laver over the egg and continue cooking until the egg sets.

5. Increase the heat to lightly brown the base. Fold the omelet in half, remove the pan from the heat, and transfer the omelet to a warm plate.

Seaside Clouds

Dried seaweed absorbs moisture when you cook it. Cooking meringue is about "drying," so laver will help the cooking process and add a delicate seaside taste. Squeaky-clean cooking utensils are important if you want to make perfect meringue.

WHAT TO USE

- ✔ 4 egg whites
- ✔ 1 cup, plus 2 tablespoons (225g) superfine (caster) sugar
- ✔ 1 tablespoon dried laver (see page 87 to find out how to dry seaweed)

Makes 10–12 large shells

WHAT TO DO

1. Preheat the oven to 225°F/110°C/90°C Fan/Gas ¼.

2. Place the egg whites in a clean bowl and use an electric whisk to beat them until they form stiff peaks. Gradually whisk in the sugar and continue whisking until the mixture is stiff and glossy.

3. Fold in the dried laver.

4. Place a small blob of meringue at each corner of a large baking tray and line with baking paper (the meringue will keep the paper in place).

5. Use a dessertspoon to heap meringue onto the baking tray, ensuring the "heaps" are well spaced out.

6. Bake in the oven for 2–3 hours until the meringues are dry and lift easily from the baking paper. Turn the tray halfway through the cooking time for an even color. Sandwich your seaside clouds together with cream if you want to or eat them as they are.

RESOURCES

FORAGING AND THE LAW

As a forager, you need to learn about the ingredients yourself; there isn't a short cut. Laws differ from country to country and can change from time to time, so please check local regulations before you start. The following websites may be useful:

UK (NOT SCOTLAND)
http://www.legislation.gov.uk/ukpga/1968/60/contents

Theft Act 1968
"A person who picks mushrooms growing wild on any land, or who picks flowers, fruit or foliage from a plant growing wild on any land, does not (although not in possession of the land) steal what he picks, unless he does it for reward, or for sale, or other commercial purpose."

Be aware of by-laws, which, in places, may remove foraging rights.

National Association for Environmental Education (UK)
http://www.nationalrural.org/organisation.aspx?id=caeafb14-5fac-42a0-9904-05cd911eb257

SCOTLAND
http://www.snh.gov.uk/enjoying-the-outdoors/your-access-rights

US
US laws regarding foraging vary at the federal, state, and city levels, and certain parks also have their own rules. Foragers in Texas should pay particular attention to state laws.

United States Environmental Protection Agency
http://www.epa.gov/lawsregs/policy/

North American Association for Environmental Education
http://www.naaee.net/

CANADA
www.gov.mb.ca/conservation/firstnations/hunting_fishing_oct_09.pdf

The Natural Resources Transfer Agreement (NRTA), which forms part of the Constitution Act, 1930, provides that Indian people "have the right, which the Province hereby assures to them, of hunting, trapping and fishing game and fish for food at all seasons of the year on all unoccupied Crown lands and on any other lands to which (they) may have a right of access." Treaty and Aboriginal rights relating to hunting, fishing and gathering are also recognized and affirmed as part of the Constitution of Canada by Section 35 of the Constitution Act, 1982.

USEFUL WEBSITES

American Museum of Natural History
http://www.amnh.org

Attenborough Nature Reserve
http://www.attenboroughnaturecentre.co.uk

Audubon Society (Birds USA)
http://www.audubon.org

Bat Conservation International
http://www.batcon.org

Beatrix Potter
http://www.bpotter.com

Boy Scouts of America
http://www.scouting.org

Bumblebee Conservation Trust
http://www.bumblebeeconservation.org

Bushcraft
* http://www.bushcraftUK.com (UK)
* http://www.bushcraftusa.com (USA)

Disabled Access
* http://www.accessibleguide.co.uk/home.php (UK)
* http://www.euansguide.com (UK)
* http://www.wheelyboats.org (UK)
* http://www.whizz-kidz.org.uk (UK)
* http://www.disabilityresources.org/PARENTS-OF.html (USA)
* http://www.easterseals.com (USA)

Earth's Endangered Creatures
http://www.earthsendangered.com/index.asp

Eilean Bàn (The Bright Water Centre)
http://www.eileanban.org

Geocaching
http://www.geocaching.com

Ghost Fishing
http://www.ghostfishing.org

Girlguiding
http://www.girlguiding.org.uk

Girl Scouts of America
http://www.girlscouts.org

Healthy Seas
http://www.healthyseas.org

International Dark-Sky Association (IDA)
http://www.darksky.org

Jake's Bones
http://www.jakes-bones.com

John Muir Trust
https://www.johnmuirtrust.org

Jurassic Coast World Heritage Site
http://www.jurassiccoast.org

Marine Conservation Society
http://www.mcsuk.org

MarLIN The Marine Life Information Network
http://www.marlin.ac.uk/index.php

Moon Phases (Northern and Southern Hemispheres)
http://www.moonconnection.com

National Geographic Kids
http://www.ngkids.co.uk

The National Trust
http://www.nationaltrust.org.uk

Natural History Museum
http://www.nhm.ac.uk

North American Mycological Association
http://www.namyco.org

The Plastic Bank
http://www.plasticbank.org

Project Seagrass
http://www.projectseagrass.org

Rachel Carson
http://www.rachelcarson.org

The Royal Society for the Protection of Birds
http://www.rspb.org.uk

The Scout Association (UK)
http://www.scouts.org.uk

Sierra Club
http://www.sierraclub.org

Slow Food
http://www.slowfood.com

The Society for the Preservation of Natural History Collections (including preserving seaweed)
http://www.spnhc.org

The Wild Network
http://www.thewildnetwork.com

The Wildlife Trusts
http://www.wildlifetrusts.org

World Wildlife Fund
http://www.worldwildlife.org

WoRMS World Register of Marine Species
http://www.marinespecies.org

The WWW Virtual Library: Mycology
http://mycology.cornell.edu

UK COURSES
* http://www.eatweeds.co.uk/about
* http://www.forageireland.com
* https://www.forestschools.com
* http://www.gallowaywildfoods.com (foraging)
* http://www.shadowhawk.co.uk (tracking)
* http://www.wildaboutpembrokeshire.co.uk (foraging)

US COURSES AND BOOKS
http://www.foraging.com

BOOKS TO READ

A Fruit Is a Suitcase for Seeds by Jean Richards
A Home for Hermit Crab by Eric Carle
A Seed Is Sleepy by Dianna Hutts Aston
Animal Skulls—A Guide to North American Species by Mark Elbroch
Bat Loves the Night by Nicola Davies
Berries, Nuts and Seeds by Diane L. Burns
Flip, Float, Fly!: Seeds on the Move by JoAnn Early Macken
Flower Fairy Series by Cecily Mary Barker
From Seed to Maple Tree: Following the Life Cycle by Laura Purdie Salas
Growing Frogs by Vivian French
Hiding in the Woods: A Nature Trail Book by Maurice Pledger
How a Seed Grows by Helene J. Jordon
Kildee House by Rutherford George Montgomery
Language of Flowers by Kate Greenaway
Little House in the Big Woods by Laura Ingalls Wilder
Lobo the Wolf: King of the Currumpaw by Ernest Thompson Seton
Lost in the Barrens by Farley Mowat
Madam How and Lady Why by Charles Kingsley
My Favorite Tree: Terrific Trees of North America by Diane Iverson
My Side of the Mountain by Jean Craighead George
My Wild Wild Kitchen by Jean Craighead George
Paddle-to-the-Sea by Holling C. Holling
Parables From Nature by Mrs. Alfred Gatty
Ring of Bright Water by Gavin Maxwell
Tarka the Otter by Henry Williamson
The Bramley Hedge Series by Jill Barklem
The Dandelion Seed by Joseph Anthony
The Tale of Peter Rabbit (and later books) by Beatrix Potter
The Water Babies by Charles Kingsley
The Wind in the Willows by Kenneth Graham
The Yearling by Marjorie Rawlings
Watership Down by Richard Adams
We're Going on a Bear Hunt by Michael Rosen and Helen Oxenbury

BOOKS FOR PARENTS
A selection of good reference books for accurate identification of plants and animals will prove useful.

A Guide to Wild Edible Plants for Parents, Grandparents, and Teachers to Use with Children by Steve Brill
The Sense of Wonder by Rachel Carson

SOME WILD APPS
BirdLog
BudBurst
Forestry Commission (cellphone/mobile apps)
Meteor Counter
Project Noah
What's Invasive
Wild Time (Project Wild Thing)

SOME GEOCACHING APPS
http://www.notaboutthenumbers.com/2012/05/11/top-5-android-geocaching-apps/

INDEX

PICTURE CREDITS

Artwork Credits
Bev Speight p.5 (dragonfly)
Rachel Boulton p.91 (seaweed pasta)

Photography Credits
All images are listed and credited where they first appear in the book.
Barbara Olive p.27 (pine)
Claire Richardson p.103 (bracelet project)f; p.103 (hanging project)
David Merewether p.15 (bees in flower), p.17 (butterfly), .47 (wild garlic), p.59 (blackberries), p.70 (caterpillar)
Debbie Patterson p.15 (snowdrop), p.47 (woodruff)
Gavin Kingcome p.5 (worms)
Getty Images:
/Adrian Myers p.126 (Pooh sticks)
/Airyelf p.52 (poppy)
/Andrey Nekrasov p.99 (squid)
/Ann & Steve Toon/robertharding p.139
/artishokcs p.81 (drawn circles)
/Arturo de Frias Photography p.46 (stag)
/Ben Queenborough p.11 (red squirrel)
/BHS p.98 (whelk)

/blackred p.3 (handprint)
/Bob Bennett p.122 (beaver)
/Borut Furlan p.99 (cuttlefish)
/Brasil2 p.99 (scallops)
/Danny James p.121 (dragonfly)
/Dave Greenwood p.39 (playing conkers)
/Dave King p.3 (sycamore seed), p.4 (acorn)
/David Courtenay p.59 (bee)
/David Merewether p.3 (starfish)
/David Tipling p.32 (growth rings), p.46 (vole), p.130 (starling)
/DEA/P. PUCCINELLI p.43 (scarlet elf)
/Dimitris66 p.95 (cucumber)
/DirchinhaSW p.121 (snail)
/Dorling Kindersley p.1 (boots), p.6 (broad green leaf), p.26 (compound leaf)
/Duncan Shaw p.124 (footprints in sand)
/Ekaterina Solovieva p.2 (green/yellow leaf), p.3 (oak leaf), p.4 (yellow/orange leaf), p.7 (yellow leaf), p.9 (slim green leaf), p.13 (yellow/brown leaf), p.25 (orange leaf)
/eli-asenova p.5 (reed mace)

/Elnur Amikishiyev p.3 (pine cone)
/Erkki Makkonen p.110 (common reeds)
/Fotosearch p.99 (lobster)
/Hans Lang p.16 (scarlet pimpernel)
/H3c7or p.3 (shell), p.72 (shell), p.73 (shell), p.100 (shells), p.101 (shells), p.103 (shells)
/jcarroll-images p.24(groups of falling leaves)
/iSpi-photography p.98 (periwinkle)
/ivanastar p.30 (bit of wood), p.31 (twig), p.32 (wood), p.33 (sticks)
/Jackie Edwards p.72 (pink seaweed)
/James Warwick p.123 (kingfisher)
/Jessica Lee/EyeEm p.47 (rabbit)
/Jim Cumming p.47 (fox)
/Joe Cornish p.99 (mussels)
/John Taylor/EyeEm p.44 (squirrel)
/Jon Boyes p.98 (limpets)
/juniorbeep p.72 (green seaweed)
/Ken Lucas p.45 (woodlouse)
/Kevin Oke p.98 (crab)
/Les Stocker p.46 (bat)
/loliputa p.2 (colored tape)
/Louise Heusinkveld p.123 (otter)
/Maisie Paterson p.99 (clams)
/Mary C. Legg p.123 (mayfly)

/Mark Hamblin p.130 (magpie)
/Matt Walford p.26 (simple Leaf)
/Mike Powles p.46 (dormouse)
/Mike Mcken p.123 (water vole)
/Otto Stadler p.15 (rabbit tracks in snow)
/Paul Kay p.79 (periwinkle)
/Paul Tourlonias/EyeEm p.44 (woodpecker)
/Peter Cade p.28 (sycamore key)
/Peter Muller p.27 (woman holding leaves)
/pialhovik p.2 (scallop seashell)
/Ray Tipper p.130 (rose-ringed parakeet)
/R A Kearton p.98 (barnacles)
/Reinhard Dirscherl p.99 (octopus)
/Richard Upshur p.110 (bull frog)
/Roel Meijer p.70 (white butterfly)
/Roman Goreilov p.5 (magnifying glass)
/Sandra Sandbridge p.123 (heron)
/Sean Gallup p.105 (sanderling)
/Tancredi J. Bavosi p.123 (dragonfly)
/Tetra Images p.26 (maple tree)
/Thomas Kitchin & Victoria Hurst/Design Pics p.123 (leaping salmon)

PICTURE CREDITS CONT.

/Tonpicknick p.98 (cockles)
/ullstein bild p.79 (starfish)
/Vic Pigula p.2 (seed head)
/Vincenzo Lombardo p.111 (grass)
/Walter Bibikow p.98 (oysters)
Gloria Nicol p.61 (rosehip)
Hybrid Images/cultura/Corbis p.8 (boy with binoculars)
iStock
/kikkerdirk p.117 (yellow frog)
/Prensis p.130 (blue tit)
Joanne O'Connell p.146 (girls in meadow)
Peter Cassidy p.119 (yellow Iris)
Peter Moore p.59 (violets), p.59 (garlic), p.59 (chickweed)
Polly Wreford p.59 (buttercup), p.68 (ladybird), p.136 (spider)

Shutterstock
/Flavored Pixels p.102 (jellyfish)
/Ken Schulze p.21 (seagrass)
/Mapichai p.50 (annotated flower)
/Mike Charles p.79 (beach scene)
/Picsfive p.75 (red pin)
/South 12th Pacific p.105 (goose barnacles)
Snap2Objects p.49 (butterflies)
Terry Benson p.10 (nature table), p.37 (trunk art), p.37 (hanging leaves), p.38 (conker furniture), p.39 (open conker), p.60 (berries), p.63 (bird feeder hanging), p.70 (boy looking under wood), p.125 (hand print), p.128 (star-gazing), p.128 (insect feeder), p.128 (snail), p.128 (cordial), p.128 (into bottle), p.129

(seaweed scone), p.132 (feeder), p.133 (kids with feeder), p.135 (wild flower water), p.137 (woodlice hotel), p.138 (all images not previously credited), p.143 (daytime star gazing), p.145 (sugar moth strips), p.155 (scones)

Every effort has been made to contact copyright holders and acknowledge sources. Any omissions will be rectified in future printings, if brought to the publisher's attention.

ACKNOWLEDGMENTS

Surrounded by the natural beauty of an Outer Hebridean Isle, it is a delightful task to be asked to write a book that encourages children to appreciate their countryside. For this opportunity I must thank Cindy Richards at Cico Books. Inspired by the great naturalist Gilbert White of Selborne, I hope that children will begin by exploring their immediate neighborhood. With encouragement a child will develop a personal relationship with our natural world, one that stretches way beyond facts assimilated in a classroom. From simple explorations and note keeping to illustrations and photographs, with persistence and patience, a nature treasure box is filled.

I must begin by thanking the children who took part in the photoshoots.

In Angus: Ellie and Robbie Towns; George, Rory, and Isaac Fyles; Fraser and Eilidh Rowan and their parents too. I am indebted to my friend Alison Preuss of The Scottish Home Education Forum, and to Dean, Dexter, and Mikey Logan; Josh York; Elana, Gabriel, and Isaac Smith; and Freddie and Jasper Wingfield-Blake. Thanks to you for building a wigwam and exploring the woods—and to your parents too.

On the Isle of South Uist: My thanks go to Hamish, Micheal, and Francis MacLellan; Dawn and Cara Steele; Izzy Francis; Anna, Katie, and Heather Campbell; and their parents too. Some of you got very wet but I never heard one complaint. My thanks also to Ella and Clara Hassells and to their amazing mother Jo, who encouraged me when this book was no more than a seed.

In London: Many thanks go to models Kevin Fernandes, Rita Lard, Sven Okpara, and Holly West.

To photographer Dylan Drummond, I say, thank you for capturing the moment perfectly while enjoying whatever the Uist and Angus weather threw at us. Some photography took place in London, so my thanks to photographer Terry Benson.

For editorial support and ever-cheerful and encouraging emails, I am most grateful to Dawn Bates and many more in the CICO Books, London office. Last, but not least, my thanks to Caroline West for her tolerance, sympathy, and endless support.

In writing this book I have pestered and been encouraged by many who include: Abi Elphinstone, Magimix UK, Jane Memmott, Kim Murray, Pete Moore, Helen Needham, George Newbery, Alison Preuss, Louise Ramsay, Fiona Robertson, Catriona Rowan, and Mark Williams.

I owe much love and gratitude to my Mother who provided encouragement and a never-ending stack of ideas. This book would, of course, not have been possible without the love and support of the usual gang, so my thanks go to: Xander, Jhonti, Lili, Alasdair, Xavier, and Maxim. It is unfair to single boys out but my nettle cordage and den builders deserve a special mention—you know who you are. Finally, and as always, I am indebted to Stephen, without whose love, patience, and cheerfulness this book would not have been written.

To all of you, thank you.

Go and run barefoot on wild thyme, a sandy beach, or on the lawn's dew. Nature will erase your footprints just as it will tidy away most of the materials used for the activities in this book.